A Year o...

by
Scott Mohnkern

A Year of Viking Rituals

A Book Published by
Scott Mohnkern
First Edition May 2009

All Rights Reserved
Copyright© 2009 by Scott Mohnkern

No part of this book may be reproduced or transmitted in any form or by any means, electronic or mechanical, including photocopying, recording, or by any information storage and retrieval system, without permission in writing from the publisher.

ISBN 1442179627

Printed in the United States of America

Table of Contents

Introduction..1
Introduction..1
The Blot...4
Tools and Participants for a Blot.................................7
   Tools...7
   Appropriate Clothing for a Blot...............................8
   The Question of Alcohol..9
   Participants in a Blot..10
The Structure of a Blot...11
   The Hammer Rite..12
   The Libation..16
The Rituals..20
   Thor Blot..21
   Freyja Blot...29
   Freyr Blot...45
   Ostara Blot...58
   Frigg Blot...72
   Sunna Blot...83
   Disablot..93
   Baldur Blot...108
   Odin Blot..118
   Tyr Blot..128
   Alfarblot...135
   Eir Blot...144
Other Rituals...152
   Sumbel...153

Weddings..156
Profession..161
Funeral..163
In Conclusion..168

Introduction

In 1973 an organization was formed in England called the Odinic rite (It was originally called the Odinist Committee). While there had been previous attempts, some as early as 1848 to recreate the religious practice of the the people of Northern Europe known as "the Vikings." The Odinic Rite started a new era in the religion now referred to as "Asatru." Since that time there have been dozens, perhaps hundreds of groups formed devoted to the worship of the gods and goddesses of Northern Europe. While there are disagreements regarding appropriate practice the ritual known as a "blot" is almost uniformly practiced by almost all of them.

This book came out of my personal desire to study this type of ritual, examining the variety that exists within practitioners. Much of what you will find here expands beyond the practices of "traditional asatru" to the general concept of heathenism.

This book is structured in three parts. The first part discusses the format of the blot (the most common ritual), including form, participants, and tools. The second contains twelve blots, one for each month of the year. The final section has other rituals that you may wish to include in your spiritual practice.

My own heathen experience began in 1997 at Free Spirit Gathering.[1] Here I met the people of Raven Kindred South.[2]. While I'd gravitated towards a heathen path for several years I'd not found my true spiritual path until I encountered this group. To them I will always be grateful for helping me with those first steps that took me to the beliefs that now consume much of my life.

With this book I start to return back to the community some of what was given me. The gods taught us that "a gift demands a gift" and this book is one small piece of the debt I owe to so many.

Special thanks go to some people:

First, my loving wife Shelly, who introduced me to Free Spirit Gathering, the Northern European path, and has always tolerated my path as she continues to follow her own. She has always been supportive of all my work as we walk the path of life together.

Second, to Lew Stead and Raven Kindred South. Without your introduction, I could not be where I am today.

---

1 http://www.freespiritgathering.org

2 http://www.ravenkindred.com

To Renee, Eve, Cat, and all the staff of Free Spirit Gathering for kicking me repeatedly to start teaching. It wasn't until I started teaching did I truly understand all the implications of that which I had learned, and that I indeed owed a gift back to the community.

And finally to the organization know as "The Blank Rune." Despite the disparities in our beliefs, we always come together in Kinship, and support each other in our tasks.

Scott Mohnkern aka "The Modern Heathen"
http://www.modernheathen.com

The Blot

The word blot (or blaut) is derived from an ancient sacrificial ritual that was practiced by Northern Europeans and Celts dating prior to the 10th century. A blot traditionally involved the sacrifice of an animal to the gods. Today this ritual is performed not by slaughtering an animal for the purpose of sacrifice, but by offering a toast in the form of mead, ale, or some other beverage in a ritualistic fashion to pay tribute to a god or goddess.

A blot is one of the core rituals for many that are on a Northern European spiritual path. Heathens typically participate in a blot at least once a month or more frequently depending upon their personal beliefs. A blot can be done within a group or individually depending upon the circumstances.

A blot is a sacrifice to a god (or goddess). It is an acknowledgement that they are an important part of our lives and the part they play in it. The ritual is designed to recognize that the gods are not just beings up above us, but are companions who bless us throughout our lives. The gods and goddess of the north are closer to us as beings than perhaps any other religious pantheon.

One important thing to note about the Northern European path is that it is an entire lifestyle. Rather than it being a tradition where one "goes to church" and then departs. The path of a heathen extends to everything we do. While the blot is ceremonial in nature, it is designed to create a condition that exists beyond the ritual itself. When we participate in a blot we're taking a piece of the spirituality that is the ritual inside us, and carry that outside the ritual into our everyday lives.

The structure of the blots that you find here are all similar with slight differences, such as the inclusion of a meditation or other items that are included for ritualistic purposes. The differences are included in the rituals here to give the reader the opportunity to see the amount of variation that can exist. As you perform these rituals, or go on to create your own, do not feel as though you need to dogmatically follow what is written within these pages. The blot you ultimately end up creating should be reflective of your beliefs, experience, and needs.

When one holds a blot, the ritual is generally short (30 minutes or less). However the ritual itself is commonly just a part of a much larger event. A feast, and perhaps a discussion or maybe a social activity (watching a movie, etc) if often a part of a typical day long event. As I present the blots here, I'll include a discussion about potential meals and discussion topics that you might want to include for your event. You'll also find a discussion of two runes with each ritual, and either a magical working or a meditation that you might also want to consider incorporating into your practice.

Tools and Participants for a Blot

Tools

A blot can be a simple ritual or a complex one involving many parts, and many tools. At the minimum, the following ritual tools to perform a blot:

- Mead, or some other beverage for which to perform a toast. This beverage is traditionally alcoholic, such as mead or ale (beer). Later we'll talk about using non alcoholic beverages in blots.
- A horn, or other vessel (Stein, Goblet, etc.) for performing the toast. Make sure if you use a horn, that it is safe for drinking beverages out of.

Any tools beyond this are entirely optional. Some other ritual tools that are used in a blot are:

- A Hlaut Bowl to pour the libation in at the end of ritual. This bowl can be metal or wood, depending upon your needs. It needs to be "free standing" so someone doesn't have to hold it during the entire ritual.
- A hammer for performing a hammer rite. Hammers are typically "two headed" and look like this:

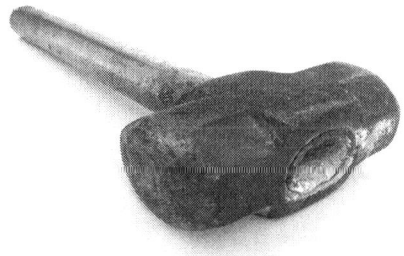

- A sprig of an evergreen tree, to asperge participants before the toasts begin.
- An attractive bottle to pour the mead into for use on the altar.
- An Oath ring, in the event someone wishes to perform an oath during the blot.
- Incense to set the mood.
- Candles, also for mood.
- A Seax (a knife). A seax normally looks like this:

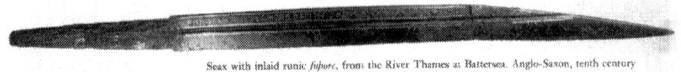

Seax with inlaid runic *futhorc*, from the River Thames at Battersea. Anglo-Saxon, tenth century

- Appropriate statuary. (Gods, Goddeses, etc.)
- A cloth for your altar.
- Items that are appropriate for the deity you are offering a blot to.

What you, or your group choose to use is entirely up to you, historically, we know very little about the tools that were used during a blot.

Appropriate Clothing for a Blot

The question of clothing (also known as "garb") for ritual comes up fairly frequently. Some recommend that you dress in appropriate "Viking Wear" (such as a tunic, lose pants, boots and an appropriate belt) while others say that it doesn't matter. The important thing with respect to the idea of ritual wear is that everyone in your group be on the same page. There are two things that one should consider; First, there is an advantage to wearing special clothing for ritual as it helps you set a proper mindset. However one could also consider the fact that the Vikings were inherently practical about what they wore for the most part, so if you're wearing common street clothes because it's "convenient" that is ok as well.

Don't feel like if you don't have your special tunic and pants that you can't do a blot. The point of a blot is to celebrate our relationship with the gods, not to hamper our ability to commune with them because its not the right time or we aren't wearing the right thing.

For my group, we normally gather week nights after work. None of us are particularly in the mood to pack viking wear into a bag and change just before the ritual, so we tend to wear normal street clothes.

However, if I'm doing rituals at a festival or large public gathering, I may very well decide to dress up and look the part.

The Question of Alcohol

The question of performing a blot with a non-alcoholic substance is an interesting one. Almost universally you'll see that some alcoholic beverage, and mostly mead or ale, is used for blots. However some practitioners, for a variety of reasons, do not use alcohol, but use a substitute such as juice or water.

Historically blots were done with Horses blood, and the transition to mead is a later incarnation of sacrifice. Mead was substituted because it was considered to be a valued commodity. So the question remains "is mead, or something alcoholic truly necessary?"

The answer is "kind of." The point of the mead is that it is a "valuable item." As we look today at things we could toast with, alcohol of any kind is typically far more expensive than water or juice. This additional cost makes it a greater sacrifice. Water or juice just doesn't have the same "value" in a society where we can literally buy any of them off the shelves for very little money.

So as you choose what you're going to toast with, consider how much value it has to you, and whether or not there might be better alternatives.

Participants in a Blot

A blot is a fairly simple ritual, so typically there are no real "qualifications" for attendance other than the desire to celebrate the god or goddess that is being celebrated. Other than the officiants everyone is "effectively the same." Some blots my require some specific hand gestures, such as making the symbol of the rune algiz. But mostly you need to be prepared to toast the deity that is being celebrated.

A modern blot generally has two officiants; the Gothi, a man, and a Gythija, a woman. The term Gothi translates from an ancient norse word meaning chief and is a sign of generic leadership rather than of religious significance.[3]

The Gothi and Gythija do not have the same roles as you'd encounter with a priest or priestess in other pagan traditions. They are primarily there as organizers to get things started and administrate the ritual.

It is not necessary to have both a Gothi and a Gythija. As you look at the blot's here there are some where it says "Gothi says..." or "Gythija says..." If you have only one officiant, they should take on both roles.

The Structure of a Blot

A blot has three core parts:

1. A Hammer Rite
2. The Invocation and Toasting
3. The Libation

Sometimes you may see additional parts added to a Blot, such as a reading or a meditation, but these three are the essential elements. Each serves its own purpose, described below.

---

3 http://en.wikipedia.org/wiki/Gothi

The Hammer Rite

What is a Hammer Rite?

Thor's hammer, Mjollnir, is the tool with which Thor fights the Jotuns (Giants). It's the means of bringing his goats back to life and is also used to bless a bride at a wedding. In other words, the hammer is an object of protection, a bringer of fertility and giver of new life. A representation of Mjollnir is commonly worn by members of the Asatru religion as an amulet.

The hammer rite establishes ritual space. This space is not as rigid as what one finds in other pagan traditions. Rather, the hammer rite is reminding us and calling to the gods, notifying them that we are about to perform a ritual. Some have described it as being similar to the ringing of a dinner bell.

When one performs a hammer rite, it doesn't create the concept of an inside and outside of ritual space. The purpose of a hammer rite is to establish that a general area is being used for ritual. It's the recognition that we're calling upon the gods and goddesses to be with us, as we exercise our will, individually and collectively, upon the universe.

If you begin all your rituals with a hammer rite it will become a matter of course and you won't have to remember to do it. Like breathing, it will become a part of your religious practice. It also gives you a brief time to focus your intent on the work you and those around you are about to be involved in.

Performing A Hammer Rite

There are many different ways to do a hammer rite:

- Some groups use two hammers and call upon two points (Ice and Fire, or North and South).
- Other groups use one hammer, and call upon two points.
- Other groups call upon four points (the cardinal directions).
- Some may just do the rite in the center of ritual space.

Commonly, there's a statement about requesting protection during the ritual, or hallowing the location.

How you choose to do a hammer rite is a matter of preference.

An easy way to do a hammer rite is to go to one of your two points, and trace an an upside-down "T" shape in the air in front of you (This is the symbol of the hammer), while chanting something appropriate like:

"Hammer of Thor, Hallow and Hold This Holy Stead".

And then go to the opposite side, and do the same thing.

Some people worry about which direction they

should trace the hammer sign in. If doing things from right to left or left to right worries you, work out to your own satisfaction what it should be. I tend to make the hammer sign from left to right, mainly because that's the direction writing goes in.[4]

After you've done one "point", then you do the others if you wish.

That's all there is to it.

The Invocation and Toasting

After the hammer rite the Gothi (or Gythija) may include a brief statement announcing the purpose of the ritual, and the deity that is being celebrated. Then the the mead is opened, and poured into the horn. In some cases, if the mead needs to "air out" before it is poured, there will be a pitcher or other container where the mead is stored beforehand.

Then the Gothi, or Gythija offers the first toast. This is done by raising the horn in the air, and then offering a toast. Toasts can be short, such as:

"Hail Thor!"

---

4 Taken from The Raven Kindred Ritual Book, http://www.ravenkindred.com/blot.htm

Or they can be longer:

> **"Thor, we thank you for the gift of rain that you have given us over the last month, we ask that you bless us by giving us the rain when it is needed, and allow Sunna her day when the we desire the warmth of the sun, Hail Thor!"**

At this point, the liquid in the horn is considered to be imbued with the essence and spirit of the god or goddess being celebrated. It is no longer "just mead" but is also spiritual and magical. As each person drinks from the horn, they are not only putting their own personal energy into the liquid and take energy and spirituality out of it.

The horn is then passed from person to person offering toasts. After everyone has given a toast the Gothi or Gythija takes the horn, which is now filled with the spirituality of every person in the ritual, and offers toast to the god or goddess being celebrated. In some cases, as people offer toasts, they may tell a story, or talk about something before they offer the toast.

Most people, when offering their toast to the god or goddess will end it with "Hail ___!" After they have said that, other participants in the ritual will normally "follow up" with "Hail ___!" after each toast.

After everyone has offered their toast, the Gothi or Gythija may do a reading or meditation. While this isn't considered standard practice it is becoming more common.

The Libation

After the reading or meditation (if there is one) there is the libation. The libation is where we take the energy in the horn and offer it to the god or goddess being toasted.

The Gothi or Gythija will then take the horn to somewhere "special" such as a tree, an area of grass, a cliff, etc. and make a brief statement and pour the remaining liquid into the ground. All other participants are invited (and in some cases expected) to join and witness the libation. A typical toast to the god or goddess being celebrated prior to a libation is as follows:

"Odin, we thank you for joining us in our stead,
We ask that you bless us with your wisdom and your knowledge as we depart this place.
We offer that which is of us to you, in tribute to you. Hail Odin!"

Some important notes:

During the passing of the horn, it is *extremely important* that the horn never be emptied. If you suspect the horn is close to becoming empty, you can politely "wave down" the Gothi or Gythija, who should be prepared to add more beverage to the horn. The reason is that the spiritual energy is contained in the liquid inside the horn, not the horn itself.

When drinking from a horn, you'll notice that the horn has a curve to the tip. As you hold it, the tip of the horn should be pointed to one side, and the curve of the horn should be toward you. If the horn is pointed away from you, or the curve of the horn is pointed away from you, the horn will fill with an air bubble, and the beverage will splash all over you.

In extremely large groups, sometimes the Gothi or Gythija may not pass the horn around from person to person, as it could literally take hours to complete the ritual. In these cases they may just offer a toast, and invite everyone to say "hail" after the toast is complete.

For those familiar with other pagan practices, some traditions believe that ritual space is something that should not be "penetrated". For example, in a wiccan circle, once the "circle is cast" participants in the ritual are not supposed to step out of, or into the circle without following a specific set of rules.

Modern heathen practice (and from what we can tell this is true historically) does not have strict rules of what "is" and "is not" ritual space. Historically we see the idea of the hof, which is similar to a modern day church or temple, participants were allowed to enter and exit without spiritual repercussions. If you attend another group's blot, they will likely advise you of rules regarding entering and exiting the ritual (for example, if you need to use the restroom), when you host your own rituals, you're welcome to make your own rules.

During a blot participants stand throughout the ritual, and positions are loosely organized. Some traditions form a circle, but many do not. Your Gothi or Gythija can tell you if there's a specific structure to where one stands.

When someone is offering a toast they are not to be interrupted. Each person is allowed their own time to speak without the interference of others. This includes stepping out for any reason. If you need to leave be sure to wait until one person is done and another starts. Also, when its your turn to speak, you shouldn't insult another participants comments.

Ritual space is celebratory in nature and doesn't have the somber feel of a Christian church. It's most times a very friendly and jovial atmosphere. There can be exceptions to this with certain types of blots, such as the Baldur blot you'll see later in this book.

The Rituals

Thor Blot

About Thor

Thor is the red-haired god of thunder. While Odin was often seen as the god of kings, Thor is the god and protector of the "common man." Thor is perhaps the most written about Norse god with many tales of his adventures. He is a revered god of Northern Europeans, both in the past and in modern times.

In addition to being protector of the common man Thor is known to bring about thunder, lightning, and rain. He carries the hammer Mjollnir, the symbol which many heathens wear as an amulet.

Historically Thor may have been the most worshiped of the Norse deities, and is also probably the most worshiped today.

About the Blot

The most common elements of a blot are in this ritual. It starts with the typical hammer rite and then goes on to a short invocation by the Gothi. This invocation is designed to bring the power of Thor into the mead. After that the round of toasts are done where each person offers a toast to Thor. It is followed up by the Gythija offering a final toast to Thor, followed by a libation.

If you are considering writing your first blot the structure of this blot is where you should start.

The Blot

Hammer Rite

Gothi takes the hammer and goes to one side of the ritual space and says:

> "We ask the gods to hallow this place as we prepare to celebrate the blessings of Thor."

Gythija takes the hammer and goes to the *opposite* side of the ritual space and says:

> "We ask the gods to protect those who have joined us to celebrate our kinship with Thor."

Invocation and Toasting

Gothi Says:

> "Great Thunderer, you who ride in a chariot drawn by goats,
>
> You who guard the bounds of midgard, who drive the frost giants back to their dark realm,
>
> You whose great hammer destroys the foes of mankind and of all life, You touch the earth with swift lightning, and the soil grows fertile, the seed sprouts when the harvest is sown, You whose mighty voice is heard across the sky, protector, defender, whose rune is most mighty to preserve, we ask you to join us today.
>
> Hail Thor!"[5]

Gothi/Gythia pass around horn, each person making their toast.

Libation

Gythija Says:

> "We give great honor to Thunor!
>
> Bane of the World Serpent, the one who struggles against the bonds of eternity.
>
> You never abandon any who call upon your name in time of trouble or crisis.
>
> Your strength and hammer keeps at bay the primal chaotic onergies known as Etins[6], those who envy the goddesses' and the gods' immortality.

---

5 Taken From Oakhedge, http://www.oakhedge.net
6 Etins is often used as an alternative word for Jotuns.

You protect us from those who would plunge Midgard into darkness and ice.

You are our defender against those who overstep their boundaries.

Those who give you honor are never abandoned; to call your name just once is to dwell in Truthheim, even in this life.

Hail Thor"![7]

Gythija pours out the horn into the hlautbowl then takes it outside, and pours it underneath a tree.

Feast Ideas for A Thor Blot

As we've talked about, Thor is the god of the common man. What better way is there to celebrate the common man than a Barbecue. So get out the grill, light it up, and have an outdoor barbecue. Ribs, hamburgers, bratwurst, hotdogs, all of it. Serving lots and lots of meat is a great way to celebrate Thor.

If you wanted to go more exotic, you could consider the tale of Thor and his goats in the Gylfaginning:

> "Thor drove forth with his he-goats and chariot, and with him that Ás called Loki; they came at evening to a husbandman's, and there received a night's lodging. About evening, Thor took his he-goats and slaughtered them both; after that they were flayed and borne to the caldron. When the cooking was done, then Thor and his companion sat down to supper. Thor invited to meat with him the

---

7 Taken From Thunder Issue 3, http://www.thorshof.org/thunder3.htm

husbandman and his wife, and their children: the husbandman's son was called Thjálfi, and the daughter Röskva. Then Thor laid the goat-hides farther away from the fire, and said that the husbandman and his servants should cast the bones on the goat-hides. Thjálfi, the husbandman's son, was holding a thigh-bone of the goat, and split it with his knife and broke it for the marrow."[8]

Goat meat can be hard to find, You could try your local exotic (Asian or Caribbean) market, or perhaps even some local Caribbean restaurants that do catering.

If you can't get goat consider going with a leg of lamb. Spice it up, put it on a spit and cook it over a big fire. Any meat that you can cook over a fire will definitely give your feast attendees that feeling of camaraderie that we associate with Thor.

Vegetables? Who needs vegetables? If you serve "meat with a side dish of meat" its all good for Thor. But if you're insistent that the all meat feast will cause your guests arteries to clog, consider classic family dishes like potato salad, mashed potatoes, or corn on the cob.

Cold beer is an excellent beverage choice. If you're a "beer snob", consider a good hefty lager. But if you're not a good all American beer will do the trick.

---

8 From the Gylfaginning, http://www.sacred-texts.com/neu/pre/pre04.htm

For dessert, again, think simple. ice cream, or apple pie are good choices. Something that is basic and simple is best. Thor isn't a big sweets god anyway.

Discussion Ideas for a Thor Blot

When we think of Thor we often see him as the "god of the masses" or the god of normal people. He is different from Odin who has a king like quality, Thor very much comes off as one of us. However he is also the god with the most physical power and the god that brings rain and thunder.

If you want to include a discussion before or after your Blot, consider including some of the following topics in your discussion:
1. Many people will offer a blot to Thor to call for good weather. Some pagan traditions believe that when you make a request like this you're asking for the opposite at some point in time to balance out the universe. If you're heathen, is this idea of cosmic balance true? When we ask the gods for a gift do we presume that the opposite of this is going to happen either somewhere else or in the future? Does the universe actually balance itself that way?
2. Of all the gods Thor is perhaps the most approachable. While he's still a powerful being he comes off like an older brother or an uncle. He also seems like the black sheep in the family. Does this

change the way you relate to him? When you offer a toast to him is it more relaxed and informal than what you might offer to Odin or Frigg?
3. Heathens, even if professed to a different god or goddess, commonly wear a hammer around their neck. Why is this symbol so important?

Runes to consider after a Thor Blot

Thurisaz (ᚦ) is a rune that many people associate with Thor. Linguistically this rune isn't tied to the god Thor. Are there reasons that this rune might be tied to Thor other than that Thor and thurisaz sound so similar? What aspects of this rune do you associate with Thor?

Algiz (ᛉ) represents the horns of the elk, and is closely tied to the concept of protection of others. Thor is seen as the protector of common man. Thinking of algiz and the idea of protecting others what role do we play? Do we have an obligation to protect others? If so, how far does that obligation extend?

Thor Meditation

Close your eyes. Think of the sound of a thunderstorm as it begins to roll over the plain. Listen to the drops of rain as they hit the ground. Feel the cold water as it falls across your face.

Stretch out your hand. The cool drops fall on your palm. You open your mouth and taste the refreshing water drip into your mouth.

Listen to the sounds of the thunder. The storm builds. You see the lightning strike in the distance. The crops glisten as the water covers them. The dry earth becomes wet, offering health to the crops.

As the storm moves in the lightning becomes brighter and the rumble of the thunder becomes louder. The storm gets closer as the rain becomes heavier.

Feel the strength of the thunder, watch the strikes of lightning as they hit around you. The rain gets harder as the storm increases.

Despite the strength of the storm the crops stand tall, resisting the onslaught. The rain continues to fall, nourishing them.

Watch, as the clouds of the storm begin to move away. The lightning becomes dim and the thunder shakes the ground less. The rain continues to fall.

The clouds slowly roll into the distance and then the sun begins to shine. You see the light of the sun warm the crops. They are stronger, and more nourished, the clouds slowly move beyond the horizon.

Feel the sun, as it warms your face, your hands, your arms, as they begin to dry. Slowly open your eyes.

Freyja Blot

About Freyja

Freyja (or Freya) is the goddess of sexual love, beauty, and the valkyries. She is described as being blue eyed, raven haired, and extremely beautiful, She is the fairest of all the goddesses, though Sif would disagree. Freyja is called on to assist in matters of sexual love, and also with respect to good seasons, albeit somewhat less than Thor. Freyja is also the goddess most closely tied to war and battle. She receives half of the dead lost in battle for her hall, Fólkvangr. She is also tied to things magical. She taught Odin the secrets of the Norse shamanic practice Seidhr, and is tied to all things magical.

Freyja is also the goddess of wealth, and is highly attracted to those things that have financial value. Many of the tales about her relate to troubles she gets into because of her desire for "bright shiny baubles".

Freyja has a brother, Freyr, who is the god of the crops. Other than Frigg, Freyja is perhaps the most honored of all the female deities in the Norse pantheon, and historically she was probably worshiped more than Frigg.

About the Blot

With this blot, we see a change in the invocation when compared with the previous ritual. In the Thor blot the invocation was just to Thor. However with this ritual we see that other deities are invited as well. In addition, while the Gothi "opened up" the blot, and the Gythija "closed" it with her libation, here we see both the Gothi and Gythija playing roles at the beginning and ending of the ritual. This can be attributed to the dualistic nature of Freyr and Freyja, who are often portrayed as "Lord" and "Lady" in other pagan religions.

The Blot

Hammer Rite

Gothi takes the hammer and goes to one side of the ritual space and says:

> "We ask the gods to hallow this place as we prepare to celebrate the blessings of Freyja."

Gythija takes the hammer and goes to the *opposite* side of the ritual space and says:

> "We ask the gods to protect those who have joined us to celebrate Freyja."

Invocation and Toasting

Gothi says:

> "We call to you, the wights of this place. Spirits of the earth, sky, or land, we welcome you. Those who are seen, and those who are unseen; all those who live in this place, we ask you to join us. Please be with us now, protect us and stand with us as we perform this ritual. Hail the landvaettir!"

All say:

> "Hail the landvaettir!"

Gythija says:

> "Honored ones, ancient ones, those who came before us, we greet you and bid you welcome. Ancestors, share your love with us, stand with us now as we perform this ritual. Be with us and grant us your wisdom. Hail the ancestors!"

All say:

> "Hail the ancestors!"

Gothi says:

> "High ones, our elder kin, we call to you, Aesir and Vanir, we bid you welcome to this place. We invite you to be with us now as we celebrate Freyja. Please stand fast with us as in the old days.
>
> Hail the Aesir! Hail the Vanir! Hail the gods!"

All say:

> "Hail the gods!":

Gythija says :

> "Lady. Vanadis. Sister to Freyr, daughter of Njord. Friend to cats, and lover to us all, we ask you to come to this place. Bearer of Brisingamen, you are welcome here. Freyja, We ask you to attend and share your love with us.
>
> Hail Freyja!"

All say:

> "Hail Freyja!"

Gothi/Gythia pass around horn, each person making their toast.

Libation

Gythija says:

> "Freyja, goddess of love, Lady of the Vanir, we toast you in recognition of the many gifts you have given us.
>
> Hail Freyja!"

All say:

> "Hail Freyja!"

Gythija drinks deeply, pour out some of the liquid into the hlaut bowl.

Gothi says :

"Freyja, we are honored to have you in our lives. We thank you for the warmth of your love, and we appreciate all that you have done for us. Hail Freyja!"

All say :

"Hail Freyja!"

Gothi drinks deeply and then pours out some of the liquid into the hlautbowl

Gythija says :

"Freyja, we are here to offer you praise as a token of our relationship to you. We ask that you receive our tribute warmly and continue to smile on us.

Hail Freyja!"

All say:

"Hail Freyja!"

Gythija drinks deeply and then pours out some of the liquid into the hlautbowl

Gothi holds up horn and says:

"This is a symbol of our gratitude to you. Please accept this offering as a gift to you. We ask that you continue to share your gifts with us. We are mindful of all that you have done, and are greatful that you will continue to smile on us.

Hail Freyja!"

All say :

>"Hail Freyja!"

Pour out remaining liquid into hlautbowl

Gythija says:

>"Freyja, Vanadis, We thank you for your presence here . We thank you for taking the time to accept our offering. We thank you once more for the gifts you bring to us.
>
>Hail Freyja!"

All say:

>"Hail Freyja!"

Gothi says :

>"Aesir, Vanir, gods of our heart, we thank you. Thank you for being here with us, and for standing witness to our offering. You are always with us, and we honor you.
>
>Hail the Aesir! Hail the Vanir! Hail the gods!"

All say:

>"Hail the Aesir! Hail the Vanir! Hail the Gods!"

Gythija says:

>"Honored ones, those who have come before, all those who are remembered, we thank you. Thank you for sharing your wisdom with us, and thank you for attending this place.

Hail the ancestors!"

All say:

"Hail the ancestors!"

Gothi says:

"Landvaettir, wights of this place, we thank you. We thank you for sharing this place with us, and we thank you for extending your protection to all that we hold dear. Thank you for being here to witness this ritual.

Hail the landvaettir!"

All say:

"Hail the landvaettir!"

Gythija takes the hlautbowl outside, and pours it underneath a tree while they both say:

Gothi and Gythija Say:

"From the gods to the earth to us,
From us to the earth to the gods.
A gift for a gift.
Hail!"

Feast Ideas for A Freyja Blot

When we think of Freyja, we think of indulgence. We should serve foods that are very rich, both in how they taste and how we see them. As opposed to the Thor feast a feast to Freyja could be a very formal sit down event where the foods are not only delicious but are beautiful as well. Here's a potential five course meal to Freyja:

Warm Lobster Salad[9]

Serves 4

- 4 T. butter
- 4 T. flour
- 3/4 cup boiling milk or fish stock
- 2 cups cooked lobster meat, chopped
- 1 egg, lightly beaten
- 1 tsp. lemon juice
- Salt
- 1 head lettuce, separated into leaves, dipped in Boiling water until wilted.
- 1 quart fish stock

Sauce:

- 3/4 cup fish stock
- 1/3 cup whipping cream
- 1/3 cup dry white wine
- 2 T. unsalted butter

Preheat the oven to 200 C (400 degrees F). Melt the butter and stir in the flour. Gradually whisk in the stock. Bring to a boil. Stir the lobster into the sauce. Whisk together the egg and lemon juice and add. Season with salt, if necessary.

---

9 From the Sons of Norway, http://www.sofn.com/norwegian_culture/showRecipe.jsp?document=WarmLobsterSalad.html

Place spoonfuls of lobster mixture on the lettuce leaves and wrap up, covering the filling entirely.

Place the lettuce leaves seam side down, in a greased baking dish. Pour fish stock over it and cover with foil and heat about 20 minutes.

Making the sauce

Combine fish stock, cream and wine and reduce by half. Cool slightly, then stir in the butter. Serve the lobster rolls hot with the sauce.

Soup – Dried Fruit Soup

Serves 10. Storage time: up to 2 days in refrigerator

- 2-1/2 c mixed dried fruit, such as apples, apricots, peaches and prunes cut into bite size pieces
- 1/2 c raisins or dried cherries
- 1/2 one lemon, thinly sliced and seeded
- 1 cinnamon stick (about 3 inches long)
- 3-1/2 c water
- 2 c orange juice
- 1-1/2 c fresh pineapple chunks or 1 1/2 c pineapple chunks packed in their own juice, drained
- 2/3 to 3/4 c honey

- 1/8 tsp salt (optional)
- 1/3 c rum or brandy
- 1 T cornstarch blended with 2 T cold water
- vanilla yogurt or sour cream

In a three quart pan, combine dried fruit, raisins, lemon slices, cinnamon stick, water and orange juice; bring to a boil over high heat. Reduce heat to medium-low, cover and simmer for 10-15 minutes. Then remove from heat and stir in pineapple, honey, salt (if desired), and rum. Let stand for 10 minutes to blend flavors and let fruit soften. Return pan to heat; then blend cornstarch mixture into soup. Cook over medium-low heat, stirring, until liquid is bubbly, clear, and thickened. Remove cinnamon stick and lemon slices. Serve soup hot; or cover and refrigerate to serve cold. Top with spoonfuls of yogurt.

Rulle Polse[10]

Serves 6-8

- 2-1/2 lbs. flanks of beef

---

10 http://www.rootsweb.ancestry.com/~wgnorway/recipe.html#Rulle%20Polse%20(Norwegian%20Meat%20Roll)

- 3 T. minced onion
- 1 lb. beef
- 1 T. pepper
- 1/2 lb. pork
- 1 T. ginger
- 1/4 lb. finely ground beef
- 4 T. salt
- 1/4 lb. finely ground pork

Trim all fat and sinews from flank. Flatten on a board. Rub in part of dry seasoning. Add the remainder and the onion to the ground meat. Spread beef and pork on a little more than half of flank, then spread on ground seasoned meat. Roll tightly and sew edges together to keep stuffing inside. Wrap tightly in a cloth. Put in a pan and cover with water. Cook slowly for about 2 to 3 hours at 375 degrees or until the inside temperature of the meat reaches 165 degrees. Remove from pan. Place between plates under a heavy weight to press out moisture and place in the refrigerator until the roll is cold. Remove cloth and slice thin. Remove threads, serve cold.

Raspberry cream[11]

Serves 4

- 1-3/4 cups whipping cream
- 4 T. sugar
- 1 tsp. vanilla extract
- 1-1/4 cup Raspberries

Whip the cream and sugar, add vanilla extract. Carefully fold in the berries, saving a few for decoration. Pour into a nice bowl and decorate with berries. Serve with almond cookies.

If you're feeling especially ambitious you could consider making, the Kvæfjord-Cake:

Step 1 - First layer of base

- 5½ ounces butter
- ¾ cup sugar
- 6 egg yolks
- 1 teaspoon vanilla sugar
- 6 tablespoons milk
- 1 cup all-purpose flour
- 1½ teaspoons baking powder

---

[11] A modification on a recipe found at http://www.rootsweb.ancestry.com/~wgnorway/recipe.html#Cloudberry%20Cream

Whisk the sugar and butter until smooth and pale. Fold in the other ingredients. Mix well. Spread on a 14 x 17 inch baking pan lined with baking/greaseproof paper.

Step 2 - Second layer of base

- 6 egg whites
- 1 cup sugar

Whisk sugar and egg whites together until stiff peaks form (meringue). Spread evenly over base made in step 1. Sprinkle 4 ounces sliced almonds on top of the meringue.

Bake the two layers together at 350 degrees Fahrenheit in lower part of the oven, for 25-30 minutes.

Step 3 - Filling

- 1 package instant vanilla pudding mix
- 1 cup heavy cream

To make the filling, whip the cream and make the vanilla pudding separately. Then mix the cream and vanilla pudding gently together, and refrigerate until cold and firm. Let the cake cool down after removing it from the oven. Cut it in half. Spread the filling on top of one half, and cover with the other. Garnish with fruit or berries.

Discussion Ideas for a Freyja Blot

1. For many pagans, Freyja is seen as a parallel to other goddesses of sexuality such as Aphrodite or Venus. However Freyja has many qualities about her that we don't see in deities of sexuality. In particular, Freyja is the goddess of warriors and taught Odin seidhr. What other aspects of Freyja make her different from other goddesses of sexuality?

2. In some of the tales regarding Freyja she agrees to trade her sexuality (i.e. have sex with someone) for material goods. While many times this turns out poorly, it is not portrayed as immoral. Is using sexuality for material gain okay from the standpoint of being a heathen?

3. Freyja taught Odin the magical skill of seidhr. However until recently Seidhr was largely a tradition practiced solely by women. What reasons might there be that Odin was give the knowledge of this tradition by Freyja?

Runes to consider after a Freyja Blot

Fehu (ᚠ) is the first rune of Freyja's Aett, and is highly associated with Freyja. It's a rune that stands for wealth, and monetary gain. Are there any other aspect of fehu that apply to Freyja?

Jera (ᛃ) is the rune that represents the profits from the harvest. Fehu generally represents the idea of wealth through ongoing activity while jera represents profits at the completion of something. Are there any other ways that jera and fehu are related to each other?

Freyja Meditation

Close your eyes. You're walking down a path through the forest. You feel the warmth of the sun as it peers between the branches of the trees. You hear the sounds of the forest as you make your way down a winding path. The path becomes narrow, the forest slowly surrounding you.

You come upon a clearing where you see two large cats. They are lying down, relaxing, barely taking notice as you approach. You observe them as they groom each other. You step closer, their heads lift, as they first notice you.

A tall raven haired woman with deep blue eyes comes from the other side of the clearing. She walks up to the cats and pets each one of them. The large cats stand up, taking their place next to her as she approaches you.

She looks at you with a smile, and says "to fill our needs is never enough, we also must fill our desires. What is it you truly desire in your life?"

She listens to you as you answer and you feel the warmth of the sun increase as you speak.

As you finish, she asks "and what price are you willing to pay for that which you desire?"

You think on it and offer her your answer. What price are you willing to pay to fulfill your desires? Is the price to much? Perhaps its not enough.

As you finish, she looks at you and says "the greater the desire, the greater the price." She and her cats turn and walk into the forest.

You walk out of the clearing the opposite direction moving back towards the path. The path winds and curves its way through the forest. You feel yourself feeling connected with the earth as you slowly open your eyes.

Freyr Blot

About Freyr

Freyr (sometimes referred to as Frey) is perhaps the most important god of the Vanir, or the "old gods". Freyr is the vanic god of agriculture and weather. He is heavily associated with fertility and is brother to Freyja. Many times you'll see Freyr and Freyja presented as "Lord and Lady." Freyr is sometimes referred to as "Yngvi-freyr."

Freyr is the god of Alfheim, the realm of the elves. He rides the dwarf created boar named Gullinbursti who glows in the dark. He has a ship by the name of Skíðblaðnir that always sails with a favorable breeze, and can be carried in a pouch if it is folded up.

Freyr falls in love and marries the giantess Gerdr but the price he pays for the marriage is to give up his own sword. He is ultimately killed by Surtr at Ragnarok.

About the Blot

This blot is perhaps the shortest of all the blot's you'll find in this book. It's here to demonstrate to you how brief a blot can be. While before we've seen blots where there invocation has taken a significant period of time, here we have a very short invocation, and then the round of toasts. It demonstrates that you don't have to have a "formal written blot" available if you know the format.

Also, with this blot each participant gives a blessing as the horn is passed around:

"May You Never Thirst"

Here we have an example of the celebration and camaraderie amongst participants in a different fashion. We're not just taking the power of the ritual into ourselves, and offering a pieces to Freyr, we're also offering a piece of our own power to the person we pass the horn.

The Blot

Hammer Rite

Gothi takes the hammer and goes to one side of the ritual space and says:

> "We ask the gods to hallow this place as we prepare to celebrate the blessings of Freyr."

Invocation and Toasting

Gothi says:

> "Freyr, god of the harvest, son of Njord, brother of Freyja, God of the Vanir, Gerd's Husband, and guardian of Alfheim. You rule the shining sun, and bless us with the fruit of the earth. We have gathered here to celebrate your blessings, as we enter the time of harvest."

All say:

> "Hail Freyr!"

Gothi fills horn with drink from vessel

Gythija says:

> "Freyr, please accept this offering in frith and plenty.
> Shine your blessings down upon this place and upon us gathered here.
> We do you honor, please accept our hospitality."

All say:

> "Hail Freyr!"

(passing it around) Gothi then toasts with the horn and passes the horn to the next person saying:

"May you never thirst."

Libation

Gothi Says:

"Freyr, Lord of frith, god of the world,
We share this drink with you in friendship.
May we share your peace and plenty."

All Say:

"Hail Freyr!"

Gythija pours out the horn into the hlautbowl then takes it outside, and pours it underneath a tree.

Feast Ideas for A Frey Blot

Freyr is the god of agriculture and the harvest How about a meal that consists of food that is grown? Rather than meat, fish, and poultry, how about trying an entirely vegetarian meal?

If you're able to grow your own food or make your own bread, providing these as part of your feast will give a personal feel to the feast and make it a part of offering to Freyr.

Here are some dishes that you could consider for a Freyr feast:

Vegetarian Tomato Soup[12]

Serves 4-6

- 6 celery stalks, including the leaves, washed, finely chopped
- 2 carrots, washed, ends removed, peeled (save the peels), finely chopped
- 1 bunch Italian parsley, washed, finely chopped
- 1 bunch beet greens and stems, washed, finely chopped
- 1 yellow onion, washed, peeled, stem and top removed, finely chopped
- 2 garlic cloves, peeled, finely chopped
- 1 large tomato, washed, stem removed, roughly chopped
- 3 tablespoons olive oil
- Sea salt and pepper
- 10 cups water

Put the chopped tomato on a cutting board or in a bowl and drizzle with olive oil and season with sea salt and pepper. Let the tomato marinate while you make the vegetable stock

---

[12] Latt, David, A Vegetarian Feast, http://menwholiketocook.blogspot.com/2009/01/vegetarian-feast.html

Heat two tablespoons of the olive oil in a large pot. Add all the celery leaves and half the stalks. Saute until lightly browned, then add the carrot peelings and half the carrots, all the parsley stems, half the beet greens and stems, half the onion, and half the chopped garlic. Stir frequently until lightly browned. Add 8 cups of water. Simmer 30 minutes. Strain and discard the vegetables. Reserve the liquid.

In the same pot, heat 1 tablespoon of olive oil seasoned with sea salt and black pepper. Add the remaining vegetables and lightly brown, about 10 minutes. Add the marinated tomato, the remaining 2 cups of water, and the vegetable stock.

Simmer 30 minutes, taste, adjust the seasoning with sea salt and pepper, and serve.

Slow Roasted Tomatoes over Croutons[13]

Makes 16-20 pieces

- 1 1/2 pounds tomatoes
- 2 to 3 tablespoons olive oil
- Sea salt and freshly ground pepper
- 1 teaspoon chopped oregano
- 1 garlic clove, minced

---

13 Madison, Deborah, Late Summer Vegetarian Feast, http://splendidtable.publicradio.org/recipes/special_vegetarian_tomatoes.html

- 4 cups croutons

Preheat the oven to 300 F. Lightly oil a large shallow baking dish. Please the croûtons on the bottom of the dish. Slice the tomatoes in half lengthwise. Set them cut side up in the dish, then brush the tops with the oil, using about a tablespoon in all. Sprinkle with salt and pepper and add the herb and garlic.

Bake, uncovered, for 2 hours. Check after an hour and drizzle a little more oil over the surfaces if they look dry.

Baked Ziti[14]

2-3 Servings

- 8 ounces whole grain ziti or other tube-shaped pasta of choice
- 8 ounces firm or extra-firm regular tofu
- 3 tablespoons nutritional yeast flakes
- 4 teaspoons freshly squeezed lemon juice
- 2 teaspoons agave nectar or brown rice syrup
- 2 teaspoons garlic powder
- 1½ teaspoons onion powder
- ¾ teaspoon dried basil
- ¾ teaspoon dried oregano

---

14 Taken from Vegan.com's 10 top recipes of 2008, http://www.vegan.com/recipes/vegancom-top-10-recipes-of-2008/baked-ziti-vegancom-top-10-recipe-2008/

- ½ teaspoon sea salt
- ⅛ teaspoon freshly ground black pepper
- 1 cup stemmed and chopped spinach
- 2 tablespoons chopped fresh parsley
- 1½ cups bottled marinara sauce or other tomato sauce of choice
- ¼ cup shredded vegan mozzarella cheese or other vegan cheese of choice

To cook the ziti, fill a large pot two-thirds full with water and bring to a boil over medium-high heat. Add the ziti and cook, stirring occasionally.

Meanwhile, crumble the tofu into a large bowl using your fingers. Add the nutritional yeast flakes, lemon juice, agave nectar, garlic powder, onion powder, basil, oregano, salt, and pepper and mash with a fork until completely smooth.

Preheat the oven to 375 degrees F. Lightly oil a 9-inch square baking pan or casserole dish. Drain the ziti in a colander and add it to the tofu mixture along with the chopped spinach and parsley. Stir until well combined.

Place half of the ziti mixture into the prepared pan. Top it with half of the marinara sauce and half of the shredded cheese. Repeat the layering procedure with the remaining ziti, marinara sauce, and cheese. Sprinkle a little additional cheese or nutritional yeast flakes over the top, if desired. Bake for 30 minutes or until heated through and lightly browned around the edges. Serve hot.

Barley Scones[15]

These tender scones are delicious plain, or topped with fresh fruit. They are made with barley flour which is sold in natural food stores and some supermarkets.

Makes 12 scones.

- ¼ cup fortified vanilla soymilk or rice milk
- 2 tablespoons maple syrup
- 1 tablespoon canola oil
- 2 teaspoons vinegar
- 1 cup plus 3 tablespoons barley flour
- ¼ teaspoon baking soda
- 1 teaspoon baking powder
- ¼ teaspoon salt
- 3 tablespoons raisins
- additional barley flour for dusting

Preheat oven to 350°F.

Mix milk, maple syrup, oil, and vinegar. Set aside.

Combine flour, baking soda, salt, and raisins in a food processor. Blend until well mixed and raisins are chopped.

Add liquid ingredients and process until a ball of

---
15 Kieswer, Kris, Healthy Eating for life, http://www.chooseveg.com/display_recipe.asp?recipe=92

dough forms.

Trasfer to a flat surface that has been dusted with barley flour. Flatten into a circle approximately 6 inches in diameter and ¾-inch thick. Use a sharp knife to score dough into 12 wedges (do not separate), then transfer to a baking sheet. Bake for 30 minutes, until lightly browned.

Discussion Ideas for an Freyr Blot

1. Today most of our eating is centered around prepared foods. Whether it be in a restaurant or that frozen dinner from the grocery store, we are no longer in a society where we grow our own crops. Does this separate us from Freyr? How can we better honor and understand Freyr if we're no longer in a position to grow our own crops?

2. While we think of vikings as meat eating hunters. However the vikings grew crops whenever they could. Why do you think the modern perception of the vikings was one where agriculture wasn't a part of their lives?

3. What other aspects to Freyr, other than being god of the harvest are important? Is there something that ties these other aspects to his role of being god of the harvest?

Runes to consider after a Freyr Blot

Hagalaz (ᚺ) represents destruction, in particular destruction due to hail or natural forces. The vikings saw that the rains, in addition to providing nutrition to their crops could become very destructive.

Much of viking philosophy describes the avoidance of overindulging in anything, as it ultimately becomes destructive. We see this in the Havamal, where it talks about drinking too much ale:

> "Less good than they say for the sons of men
> is the drinking oft of ale:
> for the more they drink, the less can they think
> and keep a watch o'er their wits. "

Hail is a symbol of when something good is overindulged in and becomes bad. What things in our lives do we overindulge in? Do we often times take things to extremes when we shouldn't? How do we learn the concept of discipline when our emotions take over?

Dagaz (ᛞ) is a rune that is very similar to hagalaz. While hagalz represents the rune of destruction, dagaz represents this destruction and rebirth. As we think about Freyr in his role of god of the harvest, how does the rune dagaz relate to his position?

Freyr Meditation

Close your eyes. You are at the base of the tree Yggdrasil. You look up, and see its branches, stretching as far as the eye can see.

At the base of the tree you see the three wells, as the norns water the base. With each ladle of water the tree grows, in every direction, expanding itself further and further, the trunk growing thicker.

You stand waiting, for what you are not sure. A barn owl comes to you and lands on one of the branches. A long tall man comes down one of the branches, and sits next to the owl. The owl flutters and perches on his shoulder.

The sun shines brightly on this man, brighter than any summer day you have seen. The sun provides healing warmth, and growth to the tree.

Then the man asks you a question:

> "How can you defend yourself, when you've given up your last weapon?"

You come up to the tree, climb up to him, then sit next to him, as you offer him your answer.

And he asks yet another question:

> "What point is there to planting the crops, when we

have to do it again every year?"

You ponder the question, and then answer him again.

The owl flutters on his shoulder, carrying your message into the sky, as you stand up, and slowly climb down the tree. As you reach its base, you look up, the tall man still there, looking down at you, as he is bathed in sunlight.

You then walk away from the tree, and slowly open your eyes.[16]

---

16 Inspired by the writings on the Northvegr web site, http://www.northvegr.org/virtual/freyr/upg/index.html

Ostara Blot

About Ostara (Also known as Eostre)

Eostre is the name of an undocumented West Germanic goddess, save the writings of the Benedictine monk Bede who described the worship of Eostre among the Anglo-Saxons as having died out by the time he began writing his Historia Ecclesiastica Gentis Anglorum in the 8th century.

Since no information regarding the figure exists outside of the mention by Bede, a number of theories exist surrounding the figure. Jacob Grimm referred to Bede when he proposed an equivalent Old High German name, Ostara, in his 1835 work Deutsche Mythologie.[17]

---

[17] Taken from Wikipedia, http://en.wikipedia.org/wiki/Eostre

About the Blot

With this blot we've added a meditation to our blot. This makes it a bit longer than most of the ones you'll find in this book. This demonstrates how you can take non traditional blot elements and incorporate them effectively into your ritual.

The Blot

Hammer Rite

Gothi takes the hammer and goes to one side of the ritual space and says:

> "We ask the gods to hallow this place as we prepare to celebrate the blessings of Ostara".

Gythija takes the hammer and goes to the *opposite* side of the ritual space and says:

> "We ask the gods to protect those who have joined us to celebrate our kinship with Ostara."

Invocation and Toasting

Gythija Says:

> "Lo, the earth awakes again
> From the winter's bond and pain.
> Bring we leaf and flower and spray,
> To adorn this happy day.
> Once again the word comes true,

All the earth shall be made new.

Now the dark, cold days are o'er,

Spring and gladness are before.

Change, then, mourning into praise,

And, for dirges, anthems raise.

How our spirits soar and sing,

How our hearts leap with the spring!

Hail Ostara!"[18]

Ostara Meditation

Gothi Says:

Close your eyes. You are walking in a dense forest. The sky is overcast and the woods are gloomy. Although occasionally a feeble ray of sunlight makes its way through the clouds and the trees. The branches of the trees are bare, although the tips are just beginning to bud. Old leaves from last year's fall scurry about your feet as an occasional gust of wind blows them about.

The ground is for the most part bare with occasional patches of snow in the shade. Hints of new green life make their way up through the snow and dead leaves.

As you walk, you notice a grove of beautiful white birches, the pale glint of their trunks and branches a pleasant contrast in the otherwise dark woods. You walk towards the birch grove and then start to walk into it. When you are surrounded by the birches, you notice a large tree that looks as if it has been struck by lightning. It's upper trunk has

---

18 Taken from Unknown original source, referenced at http://druidsegg.reformed-druids.org/newsimbolc08-15.htm

been split in two, the inner wood has been exposed to the air, dead leaves have blown their way into the nooks of the tree, in every way this tree looks as dead as it can be.

You look up from the tree, and are surprised to find a woman present. She is clad all in white, and holds a covered basket. Her gaze is steady, her eyes make you think of clear streams running in the middle of old forests, her skin reminds you of the first fair flower of spring, and her hair is long and unbound. At her feet sits a small brown hare nuzzling the hem of her skirt.

She gestures, indicating that you should come forward and you walk towards her. She points at her basket, and lifts the cloth. Inside, you see an astounding array of colored eggs, all colors, all patterns. You can think of nothing better than to pick one of these beautiful eggs, and have it for your very own.

Your hand reaches out, and she shakes her head, no. You realize that while she wants you to have an egg, she wants you to pick it sight unseen. So, you close your eyes, reach out your hand, and reach into the basket.

Eyes still closed, you draw your hand back, holding an egg. You open your eyes, and look upon your egg. What does it look like? Think to yourself what the decoration on the egg means, and why Ostara wants you to have this particular gift for the coming spring.

After you have looked at your egg, you raise your head to thank the Goddess, and she is gone. You look about for her in vain. You wonder if it has all been a dream. the reality of the egg in your hand tells you otherwise, and you know you have received the blessing of the Goddess Ostara.

As your attention moves from yourself and to the forest, you realize that the trees now have tiny, but beautifully formed green leaves at the end of their branches. And you notice that the birch tree struck by lighting, the one that looked dead, now has green shoots rising from its split trunk. As you make your way out of the birch grove, it seems that the clouds have lightened, and even as you think this, the sun comes out. Small, barely formed flowers lightly scent the forest floor, birds are singing, and the rich smell of moist earth fills your nose.

As you make your way out of the forest, you wonder how you have found the place gloomy, it seems so alive, and pleasant to walk through."[19]

Horn is passed around and toasts are offered

Libation

Gothi Says:

"For winter's rains and ruins are over and all the season of snows and sins; The days dividing lover and lover, The light that loses, the night that wins; And time remembered is grief forgotten, And frosts are slain and flowers begotten, And in green underwood and cover blossom by blossom the spring begins."[20]

Gothi pours mead into Hlautbowl, goes to a tree, and pours it into the earth

---

[19] Taken from the Raven Kindred South Ritual Book, http://www.ravenkindred.com/ostara.htm
[20] Algernon Charles Swinburne, Atalanta in Calydon

Feast Ideas for An Ostara Blot

Of all the holidays, Ostara is one of the closest to its Christian counterpart, Easter. While the Christian holiday has the rebirth of Christ as its "primary" focus. There is also the idea of the easter egg hunt and the ham. Easter is commonly a celebration of the coming of the spring. When we think of having a feast on Ostara think of dishes that focus on this idea of the "lightness" of spring.

<u>Spinach Dip & Vegetable Platter</u>[21]

- 1 envelope of vegetable soup mix
- 16 oz sour cream
- ½ cup mayonaise
- ½ tsp lemon juice
- 1 10 oz frozen package of leaf spinach
- Medium saucepan of water
- 1 red pepper
- 1 yellow pepper
- 1 zucchini
- Celery stalks
- Carrot sticks
- Fresh Broccoli

---

[21] Beltran, M.S., The Ostara: Festivities to Celebrate the Spring Equinox, http://www.associatedcontent.com/article/1476488/the_ostara_feast_recipes_to_celebrate.html

Thaw the spinach thoroughly and remove it from it's packaging. Wrap it in a clean tea towel. Over the sink, twist the ends of the tea towel, tightening it around the spinach, to drain out the excess moisture. Set it aside.

In a bowl, mix the sour cream, mayo, lemon juice and soup mix envelope. Stir in spinach. Place in refrigerator until serving.

Cut the florets off of the broccoli stems. Reserve the stems for other uses.

Bring water to boil in a medium saucepan. Add the broccoli florets for five minutes. Drain and rinse broccoli in cold water to stop cooking process. Place them in the fridge to cool.

Cut the red and yellow peppers length-wise, remove seeds and stems and cut them into sticks.

Peel the zucchini. Cut it in half. Cut the halves length-wise into sticks.

Lay broccoli florets, pepper strips, zucchini, carrot and celery sticks onto a serving tray. Serve with the spinach dip.

Deviled Eggs[22]

Makes 24 "half eggs"

- 1 dozen eggs
- 1 T. Dijon mustard
- 1/4 C. mayonnaise
- 1 t. curry powder
- 1/2 t. white vinegar
- Salt and pepper to taste
- Paprika
- Parsley, for garnish

Hard-boil the eggs and allow them to cool before peeling. Peel the eggs and slice each one in half lengthwise. Remove the yolks and place them in a bowl.

Mash the yolks up with a fork, and add the Dijon mustard, mayonnaise, curry powder, vinegar and salt and pepper. Blend it all together. Gently spoon the yolk mixture into the white halves, and sprinkle with paprika. Garnish with parsley sprigs for serving.

Lemon-Herb Roasted Leg of Lamb[23]

- 8 lb leg of lamb, bone in, trimmed of excess fat

---

[22] Wigington, Patti, Deviled Eggs, http://paganwiccan.about.com/od/ostaracooking/r/DeviledEggs.htm

[23] http://www.associatedcontent.com/article/1476488/the_ostara_feast_recipes_to_celebrate.html?cat=22

- 3 cloves of garlic
- 1 tbsp fresh rosemary leaves
- ½ cup fresh lemon juice
- 1 tbsp grated lemon peel
- 2 tbsp olive oil
- ½ tsp salt
- ½ tsp pepper
- 3 cup beef broth
- 1 tbsp extra of lemon juice
- 2 tbsp all purpose flour

Pre-heat oven to 450 degrees Fahrenheit.

Chop the garlic. Strip the rosemary off the stems and chop the leaves. Place rosemary, garlic and salt into a mortar and grind with the pestle until you achieve a paste. Stir in 2 tbsps of the lemon juice.

Paschka[24]

- 3 egg yolks, slightly beaten
- 1 cup whipping cream
- 3/4 cup granulated sugar
- 1/8 teaspoon salt
- 1 teaspoon vanilla extract
- 6 cups small-curd cream-style cottage cheese
- 1/4 cup butter or margarine, softened

---

24 http://www.recipezaar.com/Russian-Easter-Dessert-Pashka-137569

- 1/2 cup chopped mixed candied fruit
- 1/4 cup finely chopped blanched almond
- cheesecloth

Mix egg yolks and whipping cream in heavy saucepan. Stir in sugar and salt. Cook over low heat, stirring constantly, until mixture just coats a metal spoon, 12 to 15 minutes. Remove from heat; stir in vanilla extract. Place saucepan in cold water until custard is cool. If custard curdles, beat with hand beater until smooth.

Place 3 cups of the cottage cheese and 2 tablespoons of the butter in blender container. Cover and blend on medium speed, stopping blender occasionally to scrape sides, until smooth. Repeat with remaining cottage cheese and butter.

Stir custard into cheese mixture until smooth. Stir in candied fruit and almonds.

Line a 2-quart non-clay flower pot (or any form dish with openings in the bottom, like a flower pot has) with double layer dampened cheesecloth. Pour cheese mixture into pot; fold ends of cheesecloth over top. Place pot on cake rack in shallow pan; place weights on top. Refrigerate 12 to 24 hours, pouring off any liquid that accumulates in pan

. To serve, unmold onto serving plate; remove cheesecloth. Garnish as desired with additional candied fruit and blanched almonds. Refrigerate any remaining dessert.

Discussion Ideas for an Ostara Blot

1. Of all the religious holidays, the relationship between the celebration of Ostara in the spring and Easter is perhaps the most obvious. What other Christian holidays can we think of that have a close relationship with pagan ones?

2. Heathenism draws a distinction between sexuality (represented by Freyja) and fertility (represented by Ostara, Freyr and Frigg). Why do you think Heathenism draws this distinction?

3. Eggs are a very common theme in various spring rituals. Discuss how this symbol of nature is an excellent representation of the "birth of the spring."

Runes to consider after an Ostara Blot

Berkano{ᛒ) is the rune most associated with Ostara and the concept of fertility. As we think about celebrating the spring, we think about the grass growing, new animals being born, and life rejuvenating itself from a long winter.

Perthro(ᛈ) represents both the concept of the three norns and also the feminine mysteries which are closely tied to Ostara. As we think of the idea of the coming of spring how does the concept of fate and chance tie into this?

Ostara Meditation[25]

Close your eyes. You are on a grassy hillside, close to a small wood. It is a clear, sunny day. The sky is blue and birds are singing in the trees. Yesterday it rained, and in the night there was a heavy dew; so today everything is especially green and bright. There is a fresh breeze, rippling the grassy meadows and making the tree boughs gently sway. At the foot of the trees are some early flowers: daffodils and crocuses. These, too, nod their heads gently in the breeze. The trees themselves are waking up from slumber; on every branch there are opening buds, ready to break forth into bright, green leaves.

In a field nearby some sheep are grazing. Little lambs are leaping about in play, their new white fleece contrasting with the grayer coats of their mothers. As you watch, a hare scampers across the field; running fast, it soon disappears into a hedgerow.

In the valley beyond the fields is a river, sparkling clear and bright in the sunshine. Beyond there river are mountains, on whose slopes patches of yellow gorse1 blossom are showing.

Walk down towards the river; your feet swishing

---

25 http://www.sinfin.net/meditation/ostara.html

through the dew-wet grass as you go.

In the valley is a small building, like a chapel or a temple. This is your own personal temple.

Go into your temple and look around. The floor of the temple is empty, except for the small altar in its center. A bright, golden object is lying on the altar. Go nearer and examine it: it is an egg.

Pick up the egg, handle it. It feels just like an egg should: warm to the touch; neither rough nor smooth; solid, and yet fragile. The only thing remarkable about this egg is its bright, golden shell.

And yet perhaps this shell is an illusion. Look closer; it seems as though you can see inside the egg. Faint swirls of coloured light seem to come from within.

Bring your centre of awareness closer still, and you will find that you can project your consciousness right inside the egg. And now, you find yourself floating gently in a great, dark void, surronded by the brilliant pinpoints of stars and the luminous swirling masses of galactic nebulas.

One point of light, bluer and brighter than the rest, drifts closer, and you recognise it as a planet. It is our planet, the planet Earth. It draws closer and closer, until it fills almost the whole sky in front of you.

Contemplate the beauty of the globe before you. The

sea; the land; the endlessly swirling masses of cloud. The slow, but never faltering, rotation of the whole sphere under the illuminating Sun.

And now, draw back from the globe. See it grow smaller as it recedes into the distance, to be lost in an overall suffusion of golden light.

You are back in your Temple, holding a golden egg in your hand. An egg that contains the whole of the Universe that is to be. The egg, symbol of potential, creation and renewal of life, and yet it cannot exist without the creative and cherishing intelligence of the life that has gone before it. In the same way, the future of our Earth is as nothing if we do not perform our own small acts of creation and protection for the benefit of the life we live and the lives of all those creatures who share the planet with us.

Contemplate the egg for a few more moments, then replace it on the altar. Leave your Temple, closing the door carefully behind you.

You are once again on a sunny hillside, standing on the green grass feeling the fresh wind on your face. Drink in the delights of this scene and then return to reality, in the place and the time where you started your meditation. Put your consciousness in the center of your head, just behind your eyes; and when you are ready, open your eyes.

Frigg Blot

About Frigg

Frigg is said to be the wife of Odin, and is the "foremost among the goddesses". She appears primarily in stories as a wife and a mother. She is also described as having the power of prophecy yet she does not reveal what she knows.

Frigg is the only one other than Odin who is permitted to sit on the high seat Hlidskjalf and look out over the universe.

Frigg also participates in the wild hunt (Asgardreid) along with her husband.

Frigg's children are:
- Baldr,
- Höðr and,
- Wecta;

Her stepchildren are

- Hermóðr,
- Heimdall,
- Tyr,
- Vidar,
- Váli, and
- Skjoldr.

Thor is either her brother or a stepson. Frigg's companion is Eir, the gods' doctor and goddess of healing. Frigg's attendants are Hlín, Gná, and Fulla.[26]

About the Blot

As you read this blot, the form should now be pretty familiar. The Gythija opens up the space, while the Gothi offers the invocation. The purpose is that Frigg is the goddess of the heart, and it is important for those who leave the hearth, to explore the world to recognize the contribution that those who stay behind and maintain the hearth play in their lives.

The Blot

Hammer Rite

Gythija takes the hammer in the center of the ritual space and says:

> "We ask the gods to hallow this place as we prepare to celebrate the blessings of Frigg."

---

26 Edited from Wikipedia, http://en.wikipedia.org/wiki/Frigg

Invocation and Toasting

Gythija Says:

"Lady Frigg, most magnificent!
Asgard's Queen, in your cloak of stars:
We call to you: Be with us now!"

Gothi Says:

"Send your mighty maidens to us:
Swift Gna, bringing grace and good fortune;
Golden Fulla with her overflowing gifts;
Gentle Hlin, giving comfort and strong warding
Against all grief, despair and evil
That assail the heart.
Teach us your wisdom, Mother,
To order our lives, homes and folkways rightly,
For the good of all,
And to reflect your grace and brightness. [27]
Frigg I toast, Lady All-Holy,
Odin's loved companion, wonder-working queen!
Shining lady, splendid queen,
Blessed in triumph, binding folk together.
Lover of your people, lady bright-minded,
Bridler of kin-strife, bourne of kin-mindfulness.
Protector and peaceweaver, friendly goddess:
Your blessing give us, to babies and brave men,

---

27 Winifred Hodge, Source unknown.

> Mother kind, of mind most excellent.
> Great-hearted queen, holding secret counsel
> With god-loving soothsayers; to the wise-minded
> Giving rede and wisdom, discretion and prudence.
> Key-keeper mighty, in your starry cape,
> Silver adorned, shining heaven's queen!
> Bid us blithely together
> To your benches at Fen-Hall sitting;
> Offer us the cup of frith and happiness,
> Frigg, Queen beloved!
> Frigg, my beloved."[28]

Horn is passed around and toasts are offered.

Libation

Gythija says:

> "Frigg, goddess of the heart, wife to Odin, keeper of the keys, We share this drink with you in memory of the many gifts you have given us.
> Hail Frigg!"

All say:

> "Hail Frigg!"

Gothi pours out the horn into the hlautbowl then takes it outside, and pours it underneath a tree.

---

28 Friggas Web, http://www.friggasweb.org/frige.html

Feast Ideas for A Frigg Blot

When we think of Frigg we think of the home and hearth, and the comfort of the fire as we sit with our family. So why not serve "comfort foods" that we so closely associate with our family as a feast? Go to the members of your group and ask them what dish most reminds them of family, and have them bring a dish, and make it a pot luck. Here are some of my favorite dishes that remind me of home.

Home Made Macaroni and Cheese[29]

Makes 6 servings

- 1 (8 ounce) package elbow macaroni
- 1 (8 ounce) package shredded sharp Cheddar cheese
- 1 (12 ounce) container small curd cottage cheese
- 1 (8 ounce) container sour cream
- 1/4 cup grated Parmesan cheese
- salt and pepper to taste
- 1 cup dry bread crumbs
- 1/4 cup butter, melted

Preheat oven to 350 degrees F (175 degrees C). Bring a large pot of lightly salted water to a boil, add pasta, and cook until done; drain.

In 9x13 inch baking dish, stir together macaroni,

---

29 http://allrecipes.com/Recipe/Chucks-Favorite-Mac-and-Cheese/Detail.aspx

shredded Cheddar cheese, cottage cheese, sour cream, Parmesan cheese, salt and pepper. In a small bowl, mix together bread crumbs and melted butter. Sprinkle topping over macaroni mixture.

Chicken and Rice Casserole[30]

Makes 4 servings

- 1 10 oz. package of Spanish rice
- 1 10 oz. can of canned premium chicken in water
- 1 can cream of chicken or cream of mushroom soup
- 1/2 cup milk
- paprika

Cook rice as directed but simmer for only 15 minutes. (When combined with the other ingredients and cooked in the oven, the rice will cook more.)

Drain water from canned chicken. Combine soup and chicken in bowl.

Add cooked rice to soup and chicken. Stir in 1/2 cup of milk, more or less, depending on consistency desired.

Cook uncovered in a casserole dish at 350 degrees for about 20 minutes.

Bake 30 to 35 minutes, or until top is golden.

---

[30] http://www.cooks.com/rec/view/0,168,129179-251193,00.html

Ambrosia Salad[31]

Makes 10 servings

- 1 pound bag miniature marshmallows
- 2 cups broken pecans (optional)
- 1 jar (10 oz) well drained maraschino cherries(cut in half)
- 1 pound can pineapple chunks, well drained
- 1 package (7 oz) flaked coconut (optional)
- 1 can (10 oz) Mandarin orange sections, well drained
- 1 pound sour cream
- 2/3 cup mayonnaise
- 1/4 teaspoon nutmeg

Combine all of the ingredients as listed. Store in refrigerator with tight fitting lid. Refrigerate at least 4-6 hours. Do not freeze.

Discussion Ideas for a Frigg Blot

1. Frigg is known as the "keeper of the keys" and guardian of the home and family. As we consider our lives, who around us are truly our family? Many times we are either geographically or spiritually separated from our biological family, while we have much closer ties to others around us. Is it reasonable to consider these people "family" and part of your

---

31 http://www.cdkitchen.com/recipes/recs/34/Ambrosia9399.shtml

hearth?

2. In the death of Baldur, Frigg fails to protect her son Baldur from something she perceived as not a threat, mistletoe. Consider those around you, and those you protect. What you should be protecting them from? In heathenism we stress the concept of self-reliance. If we protect another, are we preventing them from becoming truly self reliant? If we are, are there things they should be protecting themselves from?

3. The concept of feminism and its role in heathen practice largely goes ignored. Many even view heathenism as sexist. Is this true? How does feminism "play out" if you are a heathen.

Runes to consider after an Frigg Blot

Othala (ᛟ) represents the physical aspects of home and hearth. In the past, there was always someone left at home to take care of things, and you knew they would always be there if you came back. Is there someone or somewhere in your life that you know, regardless of what happens, that you can always go back to and feel the protection of family?

Inguz (ᛜ) is the counterpart to othala. It represents the relationships we have with the people in our family. In today's society we may be in a position where those closest to us are not our biological family. Does this make a difference? There is an old saying:

> "you can pick your friends, but you can't pick your family."

Is this still true?

Frigg Meditation[32]

. Close your eyes and take a couple of deep breaths. Now, envision yourself standing in a clearing within a green forest. You look around, and notice the vegetation being lush and the air full of songs from various birds. The sunlight pours gently through the leaves, and gives the clearing a very peaceful atmosphere.

Take a few moments to look around.

After a bit, you notice a path leading through the trees. Curiously, you decide to follow it ...

The path leads you a good ways through the forest until you see another clearing ahead of you. Entering the clearing, you see a log-house in front you, in the center of it. The front door is slightly open, and you can see a gentle glow coming from inside. You decide to approach the door, and open it.

Just as you open the door, you hear a woman's voice

---

32 http://kokyan.com/Meditation3Eldsglor.html

from the inside, bidding you welcome and asking you to come inside.

Stepping through the door, you notice there is a fireplace at the other side of where you are standing, a table with some chairs to the side, some shelves, a stove ... and next to the fireplace sits a woman in a chair, smiling, waving you to come closer.

She bids you to sit down.

You take a moment to just look around, and take a closer look at your hostess as well.

She is wearing a linen dress, tied at the waste with a belt that bears runic symbols, holding a spindle in one of Her hands. She has a very gentle air around Her, and you immediately feel at home and comfortable being in Her presence.

She smiles at you, and introduces Herself as Frigg.

She asks you your name, and you reply ...

She bids you welcome once again, and then asks why you've come to Her house.

You state your purpose. She listens carefully, then ponders for a brief moment, and provides you with an answer to your question.

Ask Her as many questions as you please, and listen to what She has to tell you.

After all questions have been answered thank Her for Her time and wisdom.

She just smiles, and hands you a small token.

Take a moment to look at it, and then thank Her for the token.

You stand up, and make your way to the door, making sure to leave it slightly open.

You walk all the way back to the clearing you began your journey in.

Take another moment to just take in the atmosphere of the clearing, the woods around you, the sunlight, and the animals around you ...

Open your eyes, and take a moment to stretch and come to full conscious before getting up.

Sunna Blot

About Sunna

Sunna is the Norse goddess of the sun. She rides a chariot across the sky each day. In stanza 23 of Vafþrúðnismál we read :

> "Mundilfæri hight he, who the moon's father is,
> and eke the sun's; round heaven journey each day
> they must, to count years for men "

Ultimately she is devoured by the wolf Fenris.

What is most interesting about Sunna and her brother Mani are their genders. In most pagan religions (there are some exceptions) the sun is typically a male deity, and the moon female. However in heathenism the reverse is true.

About the Blot

Sunna blots are commonly done during the summer solstice, when the days are longest. Its also possible to toast Sunna at the Winter solstice, during the darkest time of the year, asking her to bring her blessings for the next season.

This blot is short. However when I have done it the "Hail Sunna's" to go on for an extended period of time. Feel free when you do this ritual, if you do it outside, to go marching "around the neighborhood" yelling "Hail Sunna" at the top of your lungs, provided you aren't disturbing your neighbors.

The Blot

Hammer Rite

Gothi takes the hammer and goes to one side of the ritual space and says:

> "We ask the gods to hallow this place as we prepare to celebrate the blessings of Sunna."

Gythija takes the hammer and goes to the *opposite* side of the ritual space and says:

> "We ask the gods to protect those who have joined us to celebrate Sunna."

Invocation and Toasting

Gothi Says:

> "To Lady Sunna! Waker and quickener of life here on Midgard.
>
> Shine down upon me/us each day so that I/we may know the joy of the days light!
>
> Shine on bright lady Sunna!"

Gythija Says:

> "It is you who give strength and nouriousment to the green growing things of this Midgard.
>
> Without this we would not have the food and subsistence we need to continue to survive!
>
> Please don't forsake your duties ever, oh great shinning Sunna! Please accept our toast to you!
>
> To bright Sunna"![33]

Gothi/Gythia pass around horn, each person making their toast.

Libation

Said by Gythija:

> "Hail To Sunna, She of the day!
>
> Sunna, Sunna, Sunna!
>
> May you grow in strength each year.
>
> Never tiring, never faltering,
>
> > mindful of the wolves at thy heels."

---

[33] Taken from the Simplified Sunday Ritual, http://www.geocities.com/volmarr/bookofshadows/asatrusimplifiedsunday1.html

Said by All

"Hail Sunna!

Hail Sunna!

Hail Sunna!"[34]

Gythija pours out the horn into the hlautbowl then takes it outside, and pours it underneath a tree.

Feast Ideas for a Sunna Blot

What you serve at a Sunna feast may largely dependent upon whether you do it in the summer or the winter. I tend to suggest that you pick dishes that celebrate the brightness of the sun. As with the Freyr feast, focusing on stuff that is "grown" works very well. Another possibility is to serve dishes that are yellow. Here are some ideas:

Southwestern Mini Corn Cakes[35]

Make 24 corn cakes

- 2 cups Sweet Kernel Corn, thawed
- 1/2 cup red bell pepper, finely diced
- 2 tablespoons parsley, chopped
- 2 tablespoons green onion, chopped
- 1 cup pancake batter, made according to package directions

---

34 Taken from Beliefnet, http://www.beliefnet.com/milestones/commemoration.asp?milestoneTypeID=4&milestoneID=37160
35 http://allrecipes.com/recipe/southwestern-mini-corn-cake-appetizers/detail.aspx

- 1/2 teaspoon salt
- 1/4 teaspoon black pepper
- 1 tablespoon butter, melted
- 1/4 cup sour cream
- Fresh chives

In a bowl combine corn, bell pepper, parsley and green onion. Stir in the pancake batter, salt and pepper. Heat a non stick skillet over medium heat. Brush pan with butter. Add heaping tablespoons of batter, cook until golden brown on each side. Remove from skillet. Place on baking sheet in warm oven, while continuing to cook remaining batter in the same way. Serve warm with small dollop of sour cream. Garnish with chives.

Spaghetti with Summer Squash and Peppers[36]

Serves 4

- 1 slice day-old whole-grain bread
- 2 1/2 tablespoons extra-virgin olive oil
- 4 garlic cloves, thinly sliced
- 1 1/2 tablespoons finely chopped walnuts
- 1/4 cup chopped fresh italian parsley
- 1 teaspoon salt
- 1 small yellow squash, cut into 2-inch julienne strips

---

[36] http://www.obesitydiscussion.com/forums/mayo-clinic-main-dishes/spaghetti-with-summer-squash-peppers-499.html

- 1 small zucchini, cut into 2-inch julienne strips
- 1 cup shredded carrots
- 1 small red bell pepper, cut into julienne strips
- 1/4 cup diced yellow bell pepper
- 1/2 teaspoon freshly ground black pepper
- 1/2 pound whole-wheat spaghetti

In a blender or food processor, process the bread to make fine crumbs. In a large nonstick frying pan, heat 1 1/2 teaspoons of the olive oil over medium heat. Add the sliced garlic and saute until lightly golden, about 1 minute. Stir in the bread crumbs and cook until lightly browned and crunchy, about 3 to 4 minutes. Transfer to a bowl and stir in the walnuts, parsley and 1/2 teaspoon of the salt. Set aside.

Add the remaining 2 tablespoons oil to the pan and heat over medium heat. Add the yellow squash, zucchini and carrot and saute until the vegetables are tender-crisp, about 5 minutes. Transfer to a plate and keep warm.

Add the bell peppers to the pan and saute until they begin to soften, about 2 minutes. Stir in the remaining 1/2 teaspoon salt and the pepper. Return the squash mixture to the pan and toss to mix. Set aside and keep warm.

Fill a large pot 3/4 full with water and bring to a boil. Add the spaghetti and cook until al dente, about 10 to 12 minutes or according to package directions. Drain the pasta thoroughly.

In a warmed shallow serving bowl, combine the spaghetti, vegetables and bread crumb mixture. Toss gently to mix. Serve immediately.

Bananas Foster[37]

Makes 2 servings

- 2 tablespoons unsalted butter
- 1/4 cup (1.75 ounces) dark brown sugar
- 1/4 teaspoon ground allspice
- 1/2 teaspoon freshly ground nutmeg
- 1 tablespoon banana liqueur
- 2 under ripe bananas, sliced in half lengthwise
- 1/4 cup dark rum
- 1/2 teaspoon finely grated orange zest

Melt butter in a 10-inch heavy skillet over low heat. Add brown sugar, allspice and nutmeg and stir until sugar dissolves. Add banana liqueur and bring sauce to simmer.

Add bananas and cook for 1 minute on each side, carefully spooning sauce over bananas as they are cooking. Remove bananas from pan to a serving dish. Bring sauce to a simmer and carefully add the rum. If the sauce is very hot, the alcohol will flame on its own. If not, using a fireplace match carefully ignite and continue cooking until flame dies out, approximately 1 to 2 minutes. If sauce is too thin, cook

---

[37] Brown, Altan, http://www.foodnetwork.com/recipes/alton-brown/bananas-foster-recipe/index.html

for 1 to 2 minutes until it is syrupy in consistency. Add orange zest and stir to combine. Immediately spoon the sauce over bananas and serve. Serve with waffles, crepes, or ice cream.

Discussion Ideas for a Sunna Blot

1. Heathenism is unusual in that the sun is represented by a female deity while the moon is represented by a male. Another example of this is Shintoism. Why do you think "the heathens" view Sunna as female?

2. In the past the warmth of the sun was seen as nothing but beneficial. This was particularly true in Northern Europe. However in today's society our view of the sun is different, and we experience many of its harmful effects as well. Does this change how we relate to the Goddess Sunna?

3. The norse had several gods and goddesses that revolved around the growing of crops even after they had begun the transition to a mercantile society. Why do you think this is the case?

Runes to consider after a Sunna Blot

Sowulo(s) is the rune that represents the sun, and the spotlight of accomplishment. As we think of the warm rays of the sun, and the feeling of warmth of gives us, think of the feeling we get when we accomplish goals and others notice them. The completion of goals is always **beneficial**, but it also "feels good" when someone takes notice. We also should notice when others accomplish their goals, providing them the "warmth of sunlight" by noticing.

Isa (↓) represents the ice and the frustration of not getting anywhere. The accomplishment of goals can help us "melt the ice" and feel like we're getting somewhere in our lives. Sometimes all we need is to accomplish a few small tasks to eliminate that feeling of being "stuck in the ice."

Sunna Meditation

Close your eyes.

Imagine you're in a deep forest in the winter. The snow covers the ground, icicles hang from the branches of the trees around you.

Feel the coldness around you, the stillness. Listen and hear the silence of the deep winter. You notice the absence of animals as you walk through the forest. All you feel is the stillness of winter.

Look up into the sky, notice that the sun begins to emerge from behind a cloud. Feel the beams of light as they peer through the forest. Watch as the snow begins to melt, providing nourishing water to the plants around you.

A small squirrel comes out from a hole in one of the trees near you and scurries up the tree. You see that he is skinny, but he has survived the long cold winter. He immediately begins to work to build his nest for the next winter.

The flowers begin to bloom, as the larger creatures of the forest appear around you. The sun becomes brighter and brighter as it reaches the top of the sky. The silence of the forest becomes active, almost noisy, as the healing power of the Sun brings the forest to life.

You continue to walk through the forest, watching as it gets ever and ever more active with the coming of the summer. You reach the end of the forest, into a field, and you slowly open your eyes.

Disablot

About the Disir

In Norse mythology, the dísir ("ladies") are fate goddesses or deities who can be both benevolent and antagonistic towards people, and they include the three norns. They could also be the protective spirits of Norse clans, and especially in connection with war expeditions, a function for which they were named fylgjas. Moreover, in later sources, the dísir also appear as Odin's shield maidens, called valkyries, and they determine the outcome of battle.

Their original function was possibly that of fertility goddesses who were the object of both private and official rituals called dísablóts, and their veneration probably derives from the worship of the spirits of the dead. A particular trait of the dísir is the fact that they appear as collective beings.

About the Blot

This is the first blot where we aren't toasting an individual god or goddess, but a group of them. This practice is unusual but not unheard of. Some individuals, when attempting to gain the blessings of the gods regarding a specific goal may offer a blot to a combination of deities, or alternatively offer sequential blots.

In addition, this blot contains a number of difficult to pronounce words and names that are in old norse. The result is that this blot can have a very ritualistic feel to it, particularly if everyone is wearing viking garb.

The following table is a quick guide to some of the more difficult pronunciations:

Capital	Lower-Case	Name	Sounds Like
Ð	ð	"ed"	"th" as in *this*, *thus*
Þ	þ	"thorn"	"th" as in *thanks*, *thrust*
Á	á		"ow" as in *owl*, *towel*
Æ	æ		"a" as in *Amy*
É	é		"ee" as in *tree*, *green*
Ó	ó		"o" as in *orange*, *order*
Ö	ö		English "o" with the lips pursed
Ú	ú		"oo" as in *toot*, *moot*

If you are relatively new to blots, this is likely to be a ritual you wish to "put at the end" of your list.

The Blot

Hammer Rite

Gothi takes the hammer and goes to one side of the ritual space and says:

> "We ask the gods to hallow this place as we prepare to celebrate the blessings of the Disir."

Gythija takes the hammer and goes to the *opposite* side of the ritual space and says:

> "We ask the gods to protect those who have joined us to celebrate the Disir ."

Invocation and Toasting

Gothi says:

> "Who are the Norns
> who are helpful in need,
> And the babe from the mother bring?"

Gythia says:

> "Of many births
> the Norns must be,
> Nor one in race they were;
> Some to gods, others
> to elves are kin,
> And Dvalin's daughters some."

Both say:

> "Thence come the maidens
> mighty in wisdom,
> Three from the dwelling

down 'neath the tree;
Urth is one named,
Verthandi the next,--
On the wood they scored,--
and Skuld the third.
Laws they made there,
and life allotted
To the sons of men,
and set their fates.

We call upon you, the norns, to celebrate with us during this time."

Gothi says:

"Then gleamed a ray
from Logafiöll,
and from that ray
lightnings issued;
then appeared,
in the field of air,
a helmed band
of Valkyriur:
their corslets were
with blood besprinkled,
and from their spears
shone beams of light.

I want Hrist and Mist
to bring me a horn,
Skeggjöld and Skögul,
Hildr and Þrúðr,
Hlökk and Herfjötur,
Göll and Geirahöð,
Randgríð and Ráðgríð
and Reginleif.
They carry ale to the einherjar."

Gythija says:

> "She saw valkyries
> come from far and wide,
> ready to ride
> to Goðþjóð.
> Skuld held a shield,
> and Skögul was another,
> Gunnr, Hildr, Göndul
> and Geirskögul.
>
> We call upon you, the Valkyries, to celebrate with us during this time."

Gothi/Gythia pass around horn, each person making their toast.

Libation

Gythija says:

> "Our fates our not just controlled by ourselves, but your actions as the web of the wyrd is weaved. We honor you, and share this drink with you in memory of the many gifts you have given us un the past.
>
> Hail The Disir!"

All say:

> "Hail The Disir!"

Gythija pours out the horn into the hlautbowl then takes it outside, and pours it underneath a tree.

Feast Ideas for a Disablot

Rarely when we think of the Disir do we think of them individually, but rather as a group. In particularly we always think of the norns as a group of three. So why not have a feast where one focuses on the number three as a tribute to all of them?

Three Bean Salad Recipe[38]

Serves 4 to 8.

- 1 15-oz can cannellini beans, rinsed and drained
- 1 15-oz can kidney beans, rinsed and drained
- 1 15-oz can garbanzo beans, rinsed and drained
- 2 celery stalks, chopped fine
- 1/2 red onion, chopped fine
- 1 cup fresh, finely chopped flat-leaf parsley
- 1 Tbsp fresh finely chopped rosemary
- 1/3 cup apple cider vinegar
- 1/3 cup granulated sugar
- 1/4 cup olive oil
- 1 1/2 teaspoons salt
- 1/4 teaspoon black pepper

In a large bowl, mix the beans, celery, onion, parsley and rosemary.

In a separate small bowl, whisk together the vinegar, sugar, olive oil, salt, and pepper. Add the dressing to the beans. Toss to coat.

---

[38] http://www.elise.com/recipes/archives/001911three_bean_salad.php

Chill beans in the refrigerator for several hours, to allow the beans to soak up the flavor of the dressing.

Turducken[39]

Serves 15-25

- 6-20 lb whole turkey
- 4-5 lb whole duckling
- 3-4 lb whole chicken (or use a larger chicken and place the duckling inside it)
- corn bread dressing
- sausage stuffing
- large roasting pan and rack
- cotton string
- large needle and cotton thread

Debone the birds:

Rinse the turkey and remove the neck and giblets. Place the turkey, breast side down, on a clean flat surface. Cut through the skin along the length of the spine. Using the tip of a knife and starting from the neck end, gently separate meat from rib cage on one side. Toward neck end, cut through the meat to expose the shoulder blade; cut meat away from and around the bone, severing bone at the joint to remove shoulder blade. Disjoint wing between second and third joints. Leave the wing bones and keep the wing attached to the meat.

---

39 http://www.thesalmons.org/lynn/turducken.html

Continue separating meat from frame, heading toward the thighbone and being careful to keep the pocket of meat on back attached to skin, rather than leaving it with the bone. Cut through ball-and-socket joint to release the thighbone from the carcass (bird will be open on one side, exposing bones left to deal with). Keep the leg attached to the meat.

Repeat boning procedure on the other side of the bird. Carefully remove the carcass and use it to make stock. Stock is needed for making stuffing and more stock is needed for gravy. To make stock, put the turkey carcass in a large pot and cover with water. Bring to a boil, then simmer on low heat overnight.

You should end up with a flat boneless (except for wings and legs) turkey with the skin intact in one large piece. Put the boned turkey in a large dish or bowl and cover with plastic wrap to keep it from drying out. Place it in the refrigerator.

Repeat the deboning process on the duckling and the chicken, but debone both stumps of wings and leg drumsticks. Cut through flesh at the thinnest point and trim around these bones with a knife until they can be removed. Both the chicken and duck will be stuffed inside the turkey and need not be kept "perfectly" intact.

Trim excess skin and fat from the birds. Ducks, in

particular, have a lot of excess fatty skin that should be saved to render fat to be used later for making gravy.

Prepare seasoning mix and set aside:

- 2 tablespoons salt
- 2 tablespoons paprika
- 1 tablespoon black pepper
- 1-2 teaspoons dried thyme

Sausage stuffing:

- 4 tablespoons butter
- 3 cups onions
- 1 ½ cups celery
- 2 lbs spicey italian sausage
- 3 tablespoons Paprika
- 3 tablespoons minced garlic
- 3 cups chicken stock.

Melt butter in large skillet over high heat. Add 3 cups onions and 1-1/2 cups celery. Saute until onions are dark brown but not burned, about 10 to 12 minutes. Add 2 lbs sausage (we prefer spicy Italian sausage) to the skillet and cook about 5 minutes or until the meat is browned, stirring frequently. Add paprika (3 tbsp.) and minced garlic (3 tbsp.) and cook approximately 3 minutes over medium heat, stirring occasionally. Stir in 3 cups of stock and bring to simmer. Continue cooking until water evaporates and oil rises to top, about 10 minutes. Stir in 2-3 cups toasted bread crumbs and mix well. Add more bread crumbs if mixture is too moist.

Prepare a similar amount of another stuffing such as corn bread stuffing.

Assembly:

At least 10 to 11 hours before dinner, assemble the Turducken.

Spread the turkey, skin down, on flat surface, exposing as much meat as possible. Rub 3 tablespoons of seasoning mix evenly on meat. Spread sausage stuffing over the turkey in an even layer approximately 3/4 inch thick.

Place duck, skin down, on top of stuffing. Season exposed duck meat with about 1 tbsp. of seasoning mix. Spread corn bread stuffing in an even layer (about 1/2 inch thick) over the duck.

Arrange the chicken, skin down, evenly on top of corn bread stuffing. Season chicken meat with seasoning mix. Spread remainder of sausage and/or corn bread stuffing on top of chicken. The assemblage will look something like this.

With another person's help, carefully lift the sides of the layered birds, folding the sides of the turkey together.

Have a helper hold the bird while sewing the opening down the back of the turkey together using cotton thread. The bird may not close perfectly, and a strip of cheese cloth can be used to help close the "crack" in the back of the turkey so stuffing will not leak out when the bird is turned over.

Since the turducken has no skeleton, it must be trussed up or it may fall apart in cooking. Tie 4-5 pieces of cotton string around the bird, widthwise to act as skeletal support. Turn the bird over and place in a roasting rack inside a large roasting pan so it is oriented breast side up and looks like a "normal" turkey. Tie the legs together just above the tip bones.

Cooking:

Heat oven to 225 degrees F. Temperature control is critical since the turducken is so massive that it has to be cooked slowly at a low temperature to prevent burning the outside before the interior is cooked. Using an oven thermometer is highly recommended. Also use a meat thermometer inside the bird to measure its internal temperature.

Place the bird in the center of the oven and bake until a meat thermometer inserted through to center reads 165 degrees, approximately 9 hours, though cooking times will vary depending on the size of the birds and amount of stuffing used. Rely on temperature and not time cooked for doneness.

There will be no need to baste, but accumulated drippings may need to be removed from the pan every few hours so that the lower portion does not deep fry in the hot oil. Save pan drippings for gravy. Remove the turducken from the oven and let cool in the pan for an hour before serving. Make gravy according to your favorite recipe or use the one below.

To serve cut bird in half. Carve crosswise so each slice reveals all 3 meats and stuffings. Will make 15 to 25 servings.

Simple Gravy:

Take 1 cup of pan drippings plus 1 cup of flour and cook over medium heat until "tan". Add 10 cups stock to fat/flour all at once. Whisk thoroughly. Bring back to a boil and then simmer for 5 min. Whisk constantly. Add salt + pepper + paprika "to taste".

Another simple gravy variation is to use about a quarter to half cup of pinot grigio and about two to three tablespoons of instant potatoes instead of the flour. Test for taste and if it gets too thick add water or more pinot.

The gravy can be made in advance and allowed to stand over low heat for at least 2 hours (maybe more).

No Bake Three Berry Pie[40]

Serves 8

- 1 - cup water
- 3/4 - cup sugar
- 2 - Tablespoons cornstarch
- 1/2 - package (4-serving size) raspberry-flavored gelatin
- 3 - cups sliced strawberries
- 1 - cup blueberries
- 1 - cup raspberries
- 1 - package (6 ounces) ready-to-use pie crust
- Whipped cream

In 2-quart saucepan, mix water, sugar and cornstarch. Over medium heat, bring just to boiling and stir constantly. Boil and stir 1 minute. Then remove from heat. Stir in gelatin until dissolved. Refrigerate about 30 minutes, stirring occasionally, until mixture thickens.

Fold berries into gelatin mixture. Pour into crust. Refrigerate about 2 hours or until set. Serve with whipped cream.

Discussion Ideas for a Disablot

1. Fate is an interesting topic for heathens. While

---

[40] http://www.alanskitchen.com/DESSERTS/Pies/No-Bake_Three-Berry_Pie.htm

there's a belief in controlling ones own destiny, there's also a strong feeling that some things are just fated to happen. The coming of Ragnarok is a perfect example of this. If we truly believe we can "change our own stars" how do we reconcile this with the idea of the web of the Wyrd and fate?

2. Heathens often believe that the path to the future is made up of ones past, and what one is doing currently. This is similar to the idea of walking a path up a mountain. When we're half way up the mountain, its just as easy to turn around and go down to the base of the mountain as it is to go to the top. However we get closer to the top, its easier just to finish the climb than it is to turn around and go back to the base. How does this apply to our future? Is it easier to change something "very far" in the future than something that is going to happen in the next 10 minutes?

3. The norse concept of time is somewhat different when compared with other pagan religions in that as opposed to the concept of "right now" they had the concept of "what's coming into being." The nature of this belief is that time is never truly static, and one cannot understand things by just looking at one moment. Why do you think the Northern Europeans

had this belief?

Runes to consider after a Disablot

Ehwaz (ᛖ) is the rune of journeying. It represents the horse. As we think about the Disir, our fate is a journey that we must take, wherever it leads us. Ehwaz reminds us that a journey is not always about the destination, it is also about how we get there and experiencing everything around us.

Nauthiz (ᚾ) represents our needs, and fulfilling them. Sometimes as we consider our fate, and where the path to the future leads we fail to focus on what we truly need out of life. Consider what you truly need in life, and how you can shape your own fate to get it.

Baldur Blot

About Baldur

Baldur is the god of innocence, beauty, joy, purity, peace, and is Odin's second son. His wife is named Nanna and his son was Brono. Baldur had a ship, the largest ever built, named Hringham and a hall called Breidablik.

Baldur, nicknamed "the beautiful", is known primarily for his death. His death and the manner of it contribute to another name for Baldur, "the slain god". His death is seen as the first in the chain of events which will ultimately lead to the destruction of the gods at Ragnarok. Baldur, however, will, as foretold in the Voluspa, be reborn in the new world.

Baldur had a dream of his own death (his mother, Frigg, had the same dream). Since the gods dreams are usually prophetic, this depressed him His mother Frigg made every object on earth vow never to hurt Baldur. All objects but one, an insignificant weed called mistletoe, made this vow. Frigg had thought it too unimportant and nonthreatening to bother asking it to make the vow. When Loki, the mischief-maker, heard of this and made a magical spear from mistletoe. He hurried to the place where the gods were indulging in their new pastime of hurling objects at Baldur, which would bounce off without harming him.

Loki gave the spear to Baldur's blind brother Hod, who then inadvertently killed his brother with it. For this act, Odin and Rind had a child named Vali, who was born solely to punish Hod, who was slain.

Baldur was ceremonially burnt upon his ship, Hringham; the hugest of all ships. Baldur's horse, with all its trappings, was burned with him. The ship was set to sea by Hyrrokin, a giantess, who came riding on a wolf and gave the ship such a push that fire flashed from the rollers and all the earth shook.

In the Elder Edda the tragic tale of Baldur is hinted at rather than told at length. Among the visions which the Sibyl sees in the prophecy known as the Voluspa is one of the fatal mistletoe.

"I behold," says she, "Fate looming for Baldur, Wodens son, the bloody victim. There stands the mistletoe slender and delicate, blooming high above the ground. Out of this shoot, so slender to look on, there shall grow a harmful fateful shaft. Hod shall shoot it, but Frigg in Fen-hall shall weep over the woe of Wal-hall."

Yet looking far into the future the Sibyl sees a brighter vision of a new heaven and a new earth, where the fields unsown shall yield their increase and all sorrows shall be healed; then Baldur will come back to dwell in Odins mansions of bliss, in a hall brighter than the sun, shingled with gold, where the righteous shall live in joy for ever more.

There is some speculation that this final section regarding the new heaven and earth being added much later than the original story, and it being in deference to Christianity. Whether or not this is the case is subject to significant debate, and deserves a book entirely on its own.

About the end of the 12th century, the old Danish historian Saxo Grammaticus tells a different story of Baldur in a form which professes to be historical. According to him, Baldur and Hod were rival suitors for the hand of Nanna, daughter of Gewar, King of Norway. Now Baldur was a demigod and common steel could not wound him. The two encountered each other in a terrific battle, and though Odin and Thor and the rest of the gods fought for Baldur, yet

Baldur was and fled away, allowing Hod to marry the princess. Nevertheless Baldur took heart of grace and again met Hod in a stricken field. But he fared even worse than before; for Hod dealt him a deadly wound with a magic sword, which he had received from Miming, the Satyr of the woods; and after lingering three days in pain Baldur died of his wounds was buried with royal honors in a barrow.[41]

About the Blot

The death of Baldur is one of the most famous tales in all of Norse literature. In this blot we've included Longellow's retelling of the tale. If you're in a group with young children this blot may not be appropriate given the topic of death.

The Blot

Hammer Rite

Gothi takes the hammer and goes to one side of the ritual space and says:

> "We ask the gods to hallow this place as we prepare to celebrate the blessings of the the dead god."

Gythija takes the hammer and goes to the *opposite* side of the ritual space and says:

> "We ask the gods to protect those who have joined us

---

[41] Modified from an article on Pagan News

to celebrate Baldur."

Invocation and Toasting

Gothi says:

"I heard a voice, that cried,
'Baldur the Beautiful
Is dead, is dead!'
And through the misty air
Passed like the mournful cry
Of sunward sailing cranes.

I saw the pallid corpse
Of the dead sun
Born through the northern sky.
Blasts from Niffelheim
Lifted the sheeted mists
Around him as he passed.

And the voice forever cried,
'Baldur the Beautiful
Is dead, is dead!'
And died away
Through the dreary night,
In accents of despair.

Baldur the Beautiful,

God of the summer sun,
Fairest of all the Gods!
Light from his forehead beamed,
Runes were upon his tongue,
As on the warrior's sword.

All things in earth and air
Bound were by magic spell
Never to do him harm;
Even the plants and stones;
All save the mistletoe,
The sacred mistletoe!

Hoeder, the blind old God,
Whose feet are shod with silence,
Pierced through that gentle breast
With his sharp spear, by fraud,
Made of the mistletoe!
The accursed mistletoe!

They laid him in his ship,
With horse and harness,
As on a funeral pyre.
Odin placed
A ring upon his finger,
And whispered in his ear.

They launched the burning ship!
It floated far away
Over the misty sea,
Till like the sun it seemed,
Sinking beneath the waves.
Baldur returned no more!

So perish the old Gods!
But out of the sea of Time
Rises a new land of song,
Fairer than the old.
Over its meadows green
Walk the young bards and sing.

Build it again,
O ye bards,
Fairer than before;
Ye fathers of the new race,
Feed upon morning dew,
Sing the new Song of Love!

The law of force is dead!
The law of love prevails!
Thor, the thunderer,
Shall rule the earth no more,

> No more, with threats,
>
> Challenge the meek Christ.
>
> Sing no more,
>
> O ye bards of the North,
>
> Of Vikings and of Jarls!
>
> Of the days of Eld
>
> Preserve the freedom only,
>
> Not the deeds of blood" ![42]

Gothi/Gythia pass around horn, each person making their toast.

Libation

Gythija says:

> "Baldur, Son of Odin and Frigg, you are wise, pure, and happy. Your death is the harbinger of Ragnarok, and your rebirth is the sign of things yet to come, we thank you for your presence with us today."

Gythija pours out the horn into the hlautbowl then takes it outside, and pours it underneath a tree.

Feast Ideas for a Baldur Blot

The pointless death of Baldur is perhaps one of the most tragic events in all of norse literature. While most feasts are festive in nature, it may be appropriate to hold a feast of a less jovial nature. One idea is to hold a dumb supper in

---

42 Henry Wadsworth Longfellow

the form of a potluck. Everyone brings a dish, and then as soon as people begin to serve themselves there should be silence. No one should talk. This allows everyone to contemplate on their own the meaning of the blot they have just participated in. It's recommended that people avoided bringing "loud foods" (like potato chips) as it interferes with the atmosphere.

Discussion Ideas for a Baldur Blot

1. The death of Baldur is partly due to Frigg's oversight with respect to protecting Baldur mistletoe. How reasonable is it for us to rely upon others when we're acting foolishly, as Baldur did by allowing people to throw objects at him? Is there a point where we need to stop relying upon others to protect us from our foolish acts, and take responsibility for them?

2. Baldur's death is a tale of a pointless death and perhaps a wasted life. Other than being beautiful, very little if anything is known about Baldur. As we contemplate our own mortality, have we wasted our lives? Will we be remembered for anything important? If not perhaps we need to consider our future actions, as death may come at any time.

3. One of the forgotten parts of the story of Baldur is Hod, and how despite his failing to know that he would be killing Baldur, is held responsible and ultimately punished and killed. What does this story tell of us with respect to the idea of personal responsibility for heathens?

Runes to consider after a Baldur Blot

Eihwaz (ᛇ) represents the tree Yggdrasil, and the idea of internal strength. In the case of Baldur, he relied solely upon his mother Frigg, to provide him with protection. Eihwaz teaches us that there are times in our lives where we cannot rely upon others to be strong and protect us. Sometimes we must protect ourselves, and part of that is not acting foolishly.

Wunjo (ᚹ) is the rune of joy. Baldur's life up until his death was pure joy. However we know very little about his accomplishments. When we consider joy, we must remember that it needs to be tempered, for if all we experience is joy, people may not remember us for anything else.

Odin Blot

About Odin

Odin is the chief god in Norse paganism. His role, like many in the Norse pantheon, is complex. He is a associated with wisdom, war, battle and death but also magic, poetry, prophecy, victory and the hunt. He brought us the runes by hanging on the tree Yggdrasil. The death of his son, Baldur is one of the signs of Ragnarok.

Other than Thor, Odin is one of the most written about gods in Norse literature.

About the Blot

In this blot we see a kenning. A kenning is a list of nicknames of which a god may go by. By examining these different names we can learn much about the god and our relationship to him. This ritual also has a balance to it in that the Gothi recites a kenning at the beginning, while the Gythija recites one at the end.

The Blot

Hammer Rite

Gothi takes the hammer and goes to one side of the ritual space and says:

> "We ask the gods to hallow this place as we prepare to celebrate the blessings of Odin."

Gythija takes the hammer and goes to the other side of the ritual space and says:

> "We ask the gods to hallow this place as we prepare to celebrate the blessings of All-Father."

Invocation and Toasting

Gothi says:

> "Odin All-Father,
> Far-Wandering Windwalker,
> Tamer of Hatred and Wearer of Ravens,
> We call on You now.
>
> Grant us the wisdom and insight
> To work with our Fate and not against it,
> To weave fridd and not fray it,

> To stand fast and not fall.
>
> Cloud-high our courage rises:
> Let us ride our Fate with the grace of Ravens.
>
> Grey-Cloaked Sage of Shifting Shapes,
> All-Seeing Eye of Magic's Might,
> Set Your shield upon us as a pledge
> That we may strive, and flourish, and fly,
> And feast with You in Valhalla
> When the last wind settles in the west."[43]

Gothi/Gythia pass around horn, each person making their toast.

Libation

Gythija Says

> "We hail you, Wodan, in all your guises –
> Wanderer, Wish-God, great giver of Wod,
> Be you Allfather, Valfather, worker of Bale,
> Strife-stirrer, Svipall, or Bileyg called,
> Helm-bearer, Wild Hunt's Leader, or Grimnir,
> By all your heitir you have my hails –
> Great are your Gifts, Great are your ways,
> and we stand tall in that which We've gained.
> We offer you this sacrifice, so that you may bless us

---

43 Taken from Circle Network News #70

with your strength, your wisdom, and your knowledge.

Hail Odin! "

Gythija pours out the horn into the hlautbowl then takes it outside, and pours it underneath a tree.

Feast Ideas for an Odin Blot

Of all the gods, Odin is perhaps the darkest, and in some ways the most "earthy" in nature. Odin is often seen as the hunter wandering through the forest. So why not serve a feast of unusual game dishes?

Goose Liver Pate[44]

- 1 lb. Goose liverwurst
- Garlic powder
- 1/2 tsp. Basil
- 1/4 c. minced onion
- 8 oz. soft cream cheese
- 1/8 tsp. Tabasco
- 1 tsp. Mayonnaise
- Olives

Make one day ahead: Mash liver with ricer. Mix in garlic powder, basil, minced onion. Cover and chill. Shape into ball.

Combine cream cheese, Tabasco, mayonnaise and garlic

---

44 http://www.cooks.com/rec/doc/0,161,154161-234200,00.html

powder; mix with fork. Put some of this mixture on the bottom of a serving plate. Place ball on top and frost with remainder of mixture. Garnish with sliced olives.

Winter Chopped Salad[45]

Serves 8 as a first course, 6 as a main course

Dressing

- 1 tablespoon Dijon mustard
- 3 tablespoons apple cider vinegar
- 1 tablespoon honey
- 1/2 cup olive oil
- Salt and freshly ground black pepper

Salad

- 1 head radicchio, cored and finely chopped
- 2 heads romaine lettuce, light green and white leaves only, finely chopped
- 1-1/4 pounds cooked chicken breasts, skin and bones removed and cut into 1-inch dice (about 3 cups)
- 1 fuji, gala, or pink lady apple, peeled, cored, and cut into 1/4-inch dice
- 1 cup dried cranberries
- 1 cup candied pecans or walnuts, coarsely chopped
- 1 cup crumbled blue or fresh goat cheese
- Freshly ground black pepper

---

[45] http://www.globalgourmet.com/food/cookbook/2007/simple-holidays/winter-salad.html

Make the dressing: In a small bowl, whisk together the mustard, vinegar, honey, olive oil, and salt , and pepper to taste. Taste and adjust the seasonings.

Place the radicchio, romaine, chicken, apple, cranberries, nuts, and cheese in a large salad bowl.

Pour the dressing over the salad and toss to coat. Sprinkle with pepper (if desired) and serve.

Advance Preparation

Make the dressing up to 2 days ahead, cover, and keep at room temperature. Whisk well before using. Make the salad up to 4 hours ahead, cover, and refrigerate.

Roast Duck[46]

Serves 2

- 5 to 5 1/2 pound duck, thawed, innards removed, wing tips removed, neck trimmed, and extra fat removed
- 4 1/2 quarts chicken stock, or three 6-ounce cans chicken broth, skimmed
- Star Anise Rub (optional, see below)
- 1/2 cup skimmed stock from duck for deglazing

---

46 http://www.cdkitchen.com/recipes/recs/260/Best-Roast-Duck101556.shtml

Remove the duck from the refrigerator. Let sit at room temperature for the 20 minutes that are needed for the next step.

Pour the chicken stock into a tall narrow stockpot. Be sure there is enough room left in the pot for the duck. By using a narrow pot, less stock is needed to cover the duck than in a wider pot. Add the wing tips, neck, giblets, and any blood from the duck. Cover the pot and bring to a boil over high heat.

Meanwhile, using the tines of a fork, thoroughly prick the duck all over, paying special attention to the fattiest areas. Insert the tines at an angle so there is a minimum risk of pricking the meat beneath. Carefully lower the duck into the boiling stock, neck end first, allowing the cavity to fill with stock so the duck sinks to the bottom of the pot. To keep the duck submerged, place a plate or pot cover over the duck to weight it down.

When the stock returns to a boil, reduce the heat and simmer 45 minutes. Even with the plate as weight, the duck will tend to float to the surface, so check about every 10 to 15 minutes to see that the duck remains submerged. Keep the stock at a gentle simmer; if it boils, the duck will rise to the surface.

When the duck has finished simmering, spoon 1 tablespoon of the duck fat off the top of the stock and spread it in the bottom of a shallow 12 x 8 x 1 1/2-inch roasting pan. Remove the plate and carefully lift out the duck, holding it over the pot to drain any liquid from the cavity. Place duck in roasting pan. Do not tuck the neck flap under the duck. Spread it out in the pan.

Pat the duck thoroughly dry and lightly coat the skin with the star anise rub(see below), gently pressing against the skin. The duck is hot and the skin is tender, so work carefully. The duck may be prepared ahead up to this point and refrigerated for a day. If made ahead, return duck to room temperature. If proceeding with roasting right away, for optimum results, leave the duck sitting out at room temperature for 30 minutes to permit the skin to dry and heat the oven to 500 degrees with oven rack on the second level from the bottom.

Place duck in oven legs first. Roast 30 minutes. After 10 minutes, spoon out the fat that accumulates in the roasting pan. Move the duck around in the pan with a wooden spatula to prevent the skin from sticking to the bottom of the pan. If it is easier, remove the pan from the oven being careful of the hot fat and spoon off fat. This will avoid getting fat on the inside of the oven, which would smoke. Make sure the oven door is closed, so that the temperature doesn't go down.

After the full 30 minutes, remove the duck from the pan. Pour or spoon off the fat, and deglaze pan with stock or water.

STAR ANISE RUB
- Scant tablespoon star anise pieces
- 1 tablespoon sugar
- 1 teaspoon mustard seeds
- 8 black peppercorns
- 1 teaspoon kosher salt

Place all ingredients for the rub in a spice mill. Process until a fine powder, stopping to shake several times for evenness. Makes 1/4 cup, enough for a whole duck.

Discussion Ideas for an Odin Blot

1. When we think of Odin with normally think of his aspects of being the wanderer and the warrior. However he's also the "owner" Valhalla, a great hall. Those who take on the mantle of Odin often find themselves also as a father figure of a large household. What are those responsibilities, and why do we take them on?

2. Odin made the great sacrifice of hanging on the tree to gain the knowledge of the runes. What sacrifices have you made for something you truly wanted? Was the price to little or too much?

3. Despite Seidhr historically being a female magical practice, Odin learned it from Freyja. There are several examples where Odin's classic maleness is tempered with traditionally female actions. Why do you think these stories appear in the literature?

Runes to consider after an Odin Blot

Ansuz (ᚠ) is known as Odin's rune and is the rune of knowledge through inspiration. Many times there is something we're trying to figure out and no matter how hard we work at it, we can't seem to solve the problem. It is only when we step back and let the problem sit, do we come up with the answer. This sudden inspiration is the "work of Odin."

Kenaz (ᚲ) is the mirror image of ansuz. While ansuz is the rune of inspiration, kenaz, the "torch of knowledge", is knowledge through study. One of the aspects of knowledge through study is that it can have drastic effects on how we perceive the world. Its important to remember that the "torch of knowledge" is not just bright, but can be destructive as well.

Tyr Blot

About Tyr

Tyr is the god of single combat, justice, and vows. He is portrayed as a one-handed man. In the late Icelandic Eddas, he is portrayed, alternately, as the son of Odin (Prose Edda) or of Hymir (Poetic Edda). Tyr is often called upon when dealing with vows or with justice.

According to the Poetic and Prose Eddas, the gods decided tried to shackle the wolf Fenris (Fenrir), but the beast broke every chain they put upon him.

Eventually they had dwarves make them a magical ribbon called Gleipnir from the noise a cat makes when it moves, the sinews of a bear, the breath of a fish, the spittle of a bird, the beard of a woman, and the roots of a mountain.

Fenris sensed the gods' deceit and refused to be

bound with it unless one of them put his hand in the wolf's mouth.

Tyr, known for his great honesty and courage, agreed, and the other gods bound the wolf. After Fenris had been bound by the gods, he struggled to try and break the rope. When the gods saw that Fenris was bound they all laughed, except Tyr, who had his right hand bitten off by the wolf. Fenris will remain bound until the day of Ragnarök. As a result of this deed, Tyr is called the "Leavings of the Wolf".

According to the Prose version of Ragnarok, Tyr is and Ggarm, the guard dog of Hel kill each other. However, in the poetic versions of Ragnarok, he goes unmentioned.

About the Blot
The Blot

This blot includes a kenning offered by the Gothi similar to the one in the Odin blot. At the end the Gythija reminds us of why Tyr is important and what he stands for. It also includes a new chant section by the Gothi of the words "Odin, Villi, Ve." Some hearths use this chant as a part of their regular ritual practice. The rest of the blot should be familiar by now.

Hammer Rite

Gothi takes the hammer and goes to one side of the ritual space and says:

> "We ask the gods to hallow this place as we prepare to celebrate the blessings of Tyr."

Gythija takes the hammer and goes to the other side of the ritual space and says:

> "We ask the gods to hallow this place as we prepare to celebrate the blessings of the Great Warrior."

Invocation and Toasting

Gothi says:

> "Tyr, God of the Morning, the horn call ends the night.
>
> Sunna wheels high over Midgard, but higher still is your might.
>
> The troops are raising banners to march in first dawn's light: Tyr, also a warrior, give us strength for the fight.
>
> Tyr, God of the Noontide, the heat makes hazy the land.
>
> Our helmets scorch our foreheads, our boots are burned by the sand.
>
> Though every step is painful, we will pursue our way;
>
> Tyr, also a warrior, help us never to sway.
>
> Tyr, God of the Sunset, the darker hours draw near.
>
> Our people are safe from dangers as long as we keep

> them clear.
>
> Before your sword and shield all shadows and foes disappear;
>
> Tyr, also a warrior, teach us to master our fear.
>
> Tyr, God of the Midnight, this battle will be our end.
>
> We always followed the North Star, for justice made our stand.
>
> If ever we were worthy for you to fight and fall,
>
> Tyr, also a warrior, lead us on to your hall!
>
> Hail Tyr!"[47]

All Say:

> **Hail Tyr!**

Gothi/Gythia pass around horn, each person making their toast.

Libation

Gythija says:

> "Tyr keeps troth with the trust of the wolf,
> with the oath of the Aesir. Angry the heath-dweller,
> Bound by the bear, by the breath of the herring,
> Maidens' mouth-hair and mountain's root,
> Caught by crow-spit and the cat-paw's din,
> Grinds in a grimace, Gleipnir straining.
> Loud is the laughter, light is the arm

---

[47] Taken from the Common Domain

Of the weakened warrior, fen-wolf's leavings".[48]

Gythija pours out the horn into the hlautbowl then takes it outside, and pours it underneath a tree.

Feast Ideas for a Tyr Blot

When one thinks of Tyr, the sacrifice of his hand is perhaps the most common story that comes to mind. Tyr is a god about keeping promises and the willingness to sacrifice for others based upon those promises. How about a potluck where everyone prepares something from food that can be given to a charity? Not only do they prepare the dish, but they also each bring goods to give to a charity afterwards. If you are doing this feast in the winter, perhaps every person can bring something for the charitable organization "Toys for Tots"[49] which is sponsored by United States Marines.

Discussion Ideas for a Tyr Blot

1. Many people reading the tale of Tyr loosing his hand to the Fenris wolf think its a story talking about the price one pays for breaking a promise. However, if you look at it closely, it is about how far we should be willing to go to keep our promises. Tyr promised Fenris his hand if the chains were not removed.

---

[48] Originally written by Math Jones
[49] http://www.toysfortots.org

They weren't removed, so Tyr gave Fenris his hand. How far are we willing to go to keep our promises?

2. Some sources say that Tyr was the original "king of the gods" who was ultimately replaced by Odin. As we look at Tyr, he often comes off as the "tired old soldier." How do we see ourselves in our community as we age?

3. Tyr is both the god of enforcing agreements and also the god of justice. Today we don't always see fulfilling promises as always being the "just thing" however the Northern Europeans did. Is keeping agreements always the just thing to do?

Runes to consider after a Tyr Blot

Tiwaz (↑) is Tyr's rune, and represents the concept of promises, oaths, and agreements. Some individuals interpret it as the rune of justice. Are there times where we are put in a position where us keeping our promises is not equivalent to justice? What if someone holds us to a promise that is a heavy burden? Why is it that Northern Europeans may have considered keeping ones promises and justice close to each other?

Uruz(ᚢ) is the rune of the Auroch, and can represent raw physical strength. This raw physical strength can grow out of control. The viking berserkers are a perfect example of the powers of uruz when they are fully unleashed. Is it appropriate in modern days for a soldier to unleash this kind of energy in a combat situation? What are the implications?

Alfarblot

About the Elves

The world of ancient paganism was hardly limited to the worship of the gods. There are various other beings who were honored, and Elf worship was often the hardest part of Paganism for Christians to destroy. It was easy enough to substitute one God for another but it was quite another to tell the common people that the elves which brought fertility to the land were not real.

Alfar are elves, Dokkalfar are dark elves which are sometimes called dwarves.[50] There are also kobolds, landvaettir, and other beings throughout the literature. While some have defined one being as doing one thing and another serving a different function, I'm not inclined to

---
50 Crossley-Holland, Kevin. The Norse Myths. London, 1980. p. xxi

draw very sharp distinctions between these various creatures. They all seem "elfish" in origin, and there seems to be no pattern of associating one name with a specific function. We know that various landvaettir or land spirits were honored with blots. We also know that Freyr is the lord of Alfheim, one of the nine worlds where the alfar are said to live.

Mythological sources tell us that the Alfar or light elves live in Alfheim where Freyr is their Lord. However, we also have the enduring belief in folklore of the elves as faery-folk. These two concepts of elves might still be linked however, as Alfheim is known to be a place of incredible natural beauty and Freyr iis an agricultural deity. To further confuse this issue, Norse folklore has a strong belief in the Landvaettir, or land spirits, who may fit into either or both of these categories. I'm inclined to lump them all together as similar beings that we simply don't know enough about to tell apart. What is important is that heathens honor the natural world and the earth very deeply. Whether one calls the spirits of the land as the elves, the faeries, or the landvaettir, or uses all of these terms interchangeably, respect to all these beings is important. Heathenism is known for having some of the most politically conservative members of the modern Pagan religions but many are staunch environmentalists.[51]

---
51 Taken in part from Ravenbok, The Raven Kindred Ritual

About the Blot

This blot does not contain any elements that we haven't seen before. The big difference here is that we're dealing with entities that definitely are not categorized as "gods." You'll also notice there's use of old Norse words similar to the Disablot.

The Blot

Hammer Rite

Gothi takes the hammer and goes to one side of the ritual space and says:

> "We ask the gods to hallow this place as we honor the spirits around us."

Gythija takes the hammer and goes to the other side of the ritual space and says:

> "We ask the gods to hallow this place as we celebrate the Alfar"

Invocation and Toasting

Gothi chants:

> "Odin Vili Ve... Odin Vili Ve.... Odin Vili Ve...."

All Join in, until it ooomo appropriate to stop.

---

book, http://www.ravenkindred.com/RBWights.html

Gythija Says:

> "Today we remember our bonds with our elder kin, the Álfar. Be they the bright Ljósálfar above, the Døkkálfar below, or the Svartálfar of the deep below. They bring us strength, wisdom, and some of our ancestrial bindings."

Gothi Says:

> "Today we remember the spirits of the land, who protect the land from those who would cause it harm. They care for the land when we cannot, and give us the blessings of the land in our lives."

Gothi/Gythia pass around horn, each person making their toast.

Libation

Gothi says:

> "The Alfar remind us of the beauty and art around us. They tell us that to work alone is never enough, that one must experience the beauty of the world around us. Today we honor you with this offering."

Gythija says:

> "The Landvaetter remind us the land is sacred, and something to be protected. They inhabit Midgard with us, and protect it as we should. Today we honor you with this offering."

Pour the remaining mead/ale from the horn into the earth, or onto a tree.

Feast Ideas for an Alfarblot Blot[52]

Most of what we find in the heathen religion is fairly grounded in "the earth." However as we approach this feast and the idea of elves we're taken into the other worlds. Some may call these the worlds of fantasy and delight. The dishes we serve at a an alfar feast should reflect the exotic nature of the beings we are celebrating. Here's a few suggestions:

<u>Ginger, Mint, and Garlic tea</u>

- Juice of 2 lemons
- 3-4 1/2 inch coins of fresh Ginger
- 1 clove of garlic
- 3 sprigs of Mint
- 2L. Filtered water, boiling
- Honey

Place Ginger, Mint and Garlic(peeled, but not crushed!) in a cheesecloth and tie off. Add to boiling water and cook for 5-7 min. Turn off heat and add lemon juice. Remove spices and transfer to an insulated tea pot. Into each cup, add a tsp. of honey(or to taste).

<u>Sauted Mushrooms</u>

- I onion, small dice

---

[52] The recipes for this feast were adapted from http://lotrscrapbook.bookloaf.net/other/recipes.html#1

- 3-4 cloves of garlic, minced
- 3 c. small mushrooms, washed
- 3 tbsp. Oil
- 1 tbsp. Thyme
- 2 c. water
- 2 tbsp. Arrowroot
- Salt&Pepper

In a medium pot or a deep pan, saute the onions and garlic in the oil until the onions are soft. Add the mushrooms and thyme and cook for two more minutes.

Add 1 1/2 c. water and simmer uncovered for 15 min. Mix the arrowroot with the remaining 1/2 c. of water, and add to pot. Cook until thickened, approx. one minute. Adjust salt and pepper to taste. Serve immediately.

Stuffed Pumpkin

- Pumpkin (about 4-5 lb.)
- 1 lb. ground beef
- 1 small onion, chopped
- 1 can tomatoes (not jumbo sized)
- 1 cup instant rice, uncooked
- 2 cups beef broth
- 4 T. butter, melted
- 1 tsp. Salt
- 1 tsp. Thyme
- 1/2 tsp. Pepper

- 1 c. grated cheddar cheese

Cut a lid in your pumpkin, scoop it out and brush the inside with the melted butter. Set it in a shallow casserole dish. Brown beef and onion together, drain. Add the rest of the ingredients *except* the cheese. Combine and scoop into the pumpkin. Put on lid. Bake pumpkin in a 350 degree oven for about 2 hours, or until pumpkin flesh is soft. About 15 minutes before it is done, take off the lid and top it with the cheese, return to oven to melt.

Serve by scooping the filling out with the pumpkin, delicious. You can save the seeds from your pumpkin to blanch and toast in the oven also.

Blackberry Tarts

Filling:

- 4 c. blackberries
- Sugar to taste
- Lemon zest to taste

Wash berries, lightly toss with sugar and lemon zest. Preheat oven to 350 degrees.

Tart shells:

- 3 c. flour
- 1 t. salt
- 1 c. butter or shortening

- 8 T. ice water (more or less)

Sift flour and salt. Cut in shortening or butter. Add cold water 1 tablespoon at a time, tossing with a fork. Shape dough into 2 balls. Roll out and cut out circles just big enough to fit the cups of a muffin tin. Fit the dough circles into the muffin pan like small pies. Fill with the berries. Bake for about 35 minutes or til pastry is lightly browned Makes about 2 dozen little muffin-sized tarts.

Discussion Ideas for an Alfar Blot

1. Politically heathens tend to be more conservative than other pagans. However you'll also find that they tend to be staunch environmentalists. The belief in the Landvaettir is part of this. Why do you think it is that heathens may have conservative views on most issues, but tend to be more liberal when it comes to environmentalism.

2. The perception of elves is largely colored by fantasy movies and books that have been published in this century. Is the modern day interpretation of these beings correct?

Runes to consider after An Alfar Blot

Raidho (ᚱ) is the rune that represents traveling to a destination. While there are some types of spiritual beings that are "with us" (such as the Landvaettier) other being reside in other worlds, and one must practice the art of Seidhr to enter them. For each individual making the decision on whether to make a journey of this type is an important one.

Mannaz (ᛗ) is the rune that represents our relationship to others. We normally think about our relationships to members of our community, and to the gods. Do we have relationships with the "beings of the land" and can we have them with the Alfar? What shape would they take?

Eir Blot[53]

About Eir

Eir is, the goddess who is called "the best of physicians" in the Edda. Eir is also counted among the Valkyries, connecting her to the ability to 'choose the slain' and awaken the dead. She is skilled at all kinds of healing, particularly herbcraft, and was even capable of resurrection.

She is one of the goddesses on the mountain Lyfia ("to heal through magic"). She was also good friends with Frigg and is listed as one of her twelve handmaidens. Eir is also the name of one of the nine maidens who serve the giantess Menglöd in the poem Svipdagsmál.

---

53 Schlosser, Michael, Eir Blot, offered at a meeting of "The Blank Rune."

About the Blot

With our final blot we add one additional element, and that's the opportunity to ask Eir for our blessing. While certainly any of these blots could contain that element, when we consider Eir, the goddess of healing, the ability to ask for a blessing is extremely important. We also include a praise in the opening. There is also a reading that can be done by anyone that is in the ritual, giving greater opportunity for participation for attendees other than the Gothi and Gythija.

The Blot

Hammer Rite

Gothi takes the hammer and goes to one side of the ritual space and says:

> "We ask the gods to hallow this place as we honor the Eir, and her healing of all those around her."

Gythija takes the hammer and goes to the other side of the ritual space and says:

> "We ask the gods to hallow this place as we celebrate the skills of Eir"

Invocation and Toasting

Gothi Says:

> "Hail healer of Asgard!
> Physician who ministers to many wounds,
> You teach us that there is never enough healing,
> Never enough time, never enough resources,
> Never enough hope that anything will survive,
> And yet even in face of this helplessness.
> You teach us that we must go on,
> And never give up until the end.
> And this is the wound of creation,
> that can never be healed
> And yet we must keep trying.
> For perseverance is more than merely stubbornness,
> It is the living embodiment of hope.
> We invite you to join us here today, in your honor."

Reading – Eir's Song of Healing

Anyone may read

> "The soft-weeping moon clings to her indifference,
> As my soul caresses your fevered brow.
> Moan not in unison with the gust-driven tempests,
> But trust in my comforting touch.
> The stars, their pinions of made of twilight,
> Fly to the moon and beg healing for you.

The moon remains unmoved- ah, pitilous orb-
But I have come to your side.
Now surrender to the mild chant of a lullaby
As soft as the sighs of the gods.
I shall heal your mortal bonds made of flesh,
And I shall free you from torment's grip.
The provoking pangs of anguish,
Caused by pain's own merciless soul,
Shall flee in shades of bewildered confusion,
As I stand by your trembling side.
I shall console your soul as you sleep,
And flesh shall mend, bones shall heal,
And though the moon hides her mercy
From the gold-swept stars and their pleadings,
All good peace shall be restored to you."

Instead of the normal Toast, please feel free to take this time to ask for Eir to take an active hand in either someone's wellness, or in their training in becoming a physician.

Libation

Gythija Says:

"Eir, whose loving hands and sweet breath brings healing and health. We thank you for your gentle caress, your soft ministrations and your care. When stress, strains, aches and pains plague is, you come with your lithe figure and flowing hair to ease our distress. Thank you for assisting us here in Midgard, both tonite and the rest of the year. Eir, goddess holy and wise, we honor you. Hail Eir!"

All say:

"Hail Eir!"

Gothi then pours the remaining liquid from the horn into the hlautbowl, and then takes it outside and pours it out into the earth.

Feast Ideas for an Eir Blot

Eir is the goddess of healing, and the best place to start with healing is to eat properly to keep ourselves healthy to begin with. We can honor her by placing ourselves in a position where we are healthy to begin with. Here are a few dishes that are considered especially healthy.

Asapargus Guacamole[54]

- 24 spears fresh asparagus, trimmed and coarsely chopped
- 1/2 cup salsa
- 1 tablespoon chopped cilantro
- 2 cloves garlic
- 4 green onions, sliced

Place the asparagus in a pot with enough water to cover. Bring to a boil, and cook 5 minutes, until tender but firm. Drain, and rinse with cold water.

---

54 Peabody, http://allrecipes.com/Recipe/Asparagus-Guacamole/Detail.aspx

Place the asparagus, salsa, cilantro, garlic, and green onions in a food processor or blender, and process to desired consistency. Refrigerate 1 hour, or until chilled, before serving with tortilla chips.

Strawberry Spinach Salad[55]

- 2 tablespoons sesame seeds
- 1 tablespoon poppy seeds
- 1/2 cup white sugar
- 1/2 cup olive oil
- 1/4 cup distilled white vinegar
- 1/4 teaspoon paprika
- 1/4 teaspoon Worcestershire sauce
- 1 tablespoon minced onion
- 10 ounces fresh spinach - rinsed, dried and torn into bite-size pieces
- 1 quart strawberries - cleaned, hulled and sliced
- 1/4 cup almonds, blanched and slivered

In a medium bowl, whisk together the sesame seeds, poppy seeds, sugar, olive oil, vinegar, paprika, Worcestershire sauce and onion. Cover, and chill for one hour.

In a large bowl, combine the spinach, strawberries and almonds. Pour dressing over salad, and toss. Refrigerate 10 to 15 minutes before serving.

---

[55] http://allrecipes.com/Recipe/Strawberry-Spinach-Salad/Detail.aspx

Pasta with Lentil Soup Sauce

- 1 (16 ounce) package uncooked spaghetti
- 2 (19 ounce) cans lentil soup
- freshly ground black pepper to taste

Bring a large pot of lightly salted water to a boil. Add spaghetti and cook for 8 to 10 minutes or until al dente; drain, but do not rinse, and return to pot. Stir in lentil soup and season with black pepper. Heat through and serve.

Discussion Ideas for an Eir Blot

1. Eir's approach to healing is often described as "gentler and slower." How does this compare to the way with the way we think about medicine now? Are we better off taking a slow approach to resolving our health issues rather than getting them fixed immediately?

2. Eir only taught women her healing powers. Do you think that is true today? If so, if you're a male in a medical profession, what god or goddess would you go to for guidance?

Runes to consider after An Eir Blot

Laguz (ᛚ) represents the lake, and the power of healing. Even today much of what "ails us" can be dealt with using the power of water. Whether it be cleaning out a cut, or healing our kidneys by drinking more water. Water has an incredible power of healing that we often don't consider.

Gebo (X) represents the gift. History teaches us that a "gift demands a gift." If we're given the precious gift of healing, we have an obligation to share that gift with others. However, how far does this obligation extend? Many people who have the gift of healing find themselves exhausted because they are constantly using it. Is there a point where we have to make a decision that our societal obligation to share our gifts ends? How do we decide where that is?

Other Rituals

Sumbel

One of the most common celebrations noted in tales of the vikings is the sumbel, or ritual drinking celebration.

The sumbel and blot are two sides of the same coin. A blot is a ritual to enhance the relationship between ourselves and the gods/goddesses. A sumbel, while certainly strengthening our bonds with the gods, is more about strengthening the bond in our community. A sumbel is more "mundane" (less religious) than a blot, but in many ways is more significant.

Guests are seated and the host begins with a short statement of greeting and intent, and then offers the first toast. The horn is then passed around the table and each person makes their toasts in turn. At a sumbel toasts are drunk to the gods as well as to a persons ancestors or personal heroes. Rather than a toast, a person might also offer a brag or some story, song, or poem that has significance. The importance is that at the end of the toast, story, or whatever, the person offering it drinks from the horn, and in doing so "drinks in" what he spoke.

The sumbel is an important time for people to get to know each other in a more intimate way than most people are willing to share. People within our modern society often behave at one of two extremes. At one end are individuals who remain distant from others, either because to display emotion would be inappropriate or because they have been socialized to believe that "keeping a distance from others" is the only desirable way to live. On the other side are those who cultivate their "feelings" and who spend their lives consciously attempting to stir their emotions and force an unnatural level of intimacy between themselves and others. There are some levels of emotional intimacy which are not meant to be openly shared with strangers. Doing so reduces their meaning to the mundane. At sumbel, barriers can be lowered in a place which is sacred to the Gods. Thoughts can be shared among companions and friends without embarrassment or forced intimacy.

One format for the sumbel is to drink three rounds. The first is dedicated to the Gods, the second to ancestors, and the third to personal ancestors, heroes, or friends which have passed from this world. An alternative to this is for the first round to be to the gods, the second to an ancestor who has passed on, and the third a personal boast.

Another format is "past, present, and future." This type of sumbel is more of a magical ritual than one of celebration. The idea is to make toasts which bring up some aspect of your past and present situation, and a third toast or brag which represents your wishes for the future. One might make a toast to the first ritual one attended as the past, a second to the companions and kindred then gathered, and for his third toast might state that he intends to be dedicate himself as a Gothi in the coming year. The purpose would be to link the coming event of his dedication with the two already accomplished events of pledging heathenism and finding a kindred -- two other important rites of passage. In this case initiation as a Gothi then becomes something which is linked to a chain of events that have already occurred, rather than an isolated action which might occur. Thus magically, this moves the person towards his goal.

A third and ever popular type of sumbel is a free-for-all where stories are told, toasts are made and bragging is done until all gathered are under the table. Perhaps this is not quite so esoteric or purposeful as the previous ideas, but it's certainly in keeping with the examples of our Gods and ancestors. In any case, no matter how relaxed a sumbel has become, I have never seen one that was merely a drinking event. Some of the most intense experiences I have had with people have come from such "open ended" sumbels.

Weddings[56]

In terms of structure, there's little historical information that we have regarding weddings other than that they existed. We do know that marriage was as much about a financial relationship as it was a romantic one. Heathens who choose to get married often end up designing their own rituals. Here's some basic information that may help you out if you are ever in a position to need a heathen wedding.

- The most important element of a heathen wedding is the blessing of the bride with the hammer. Traditionally, the bride is seated, and after signing her with the hammer (making the sign of the hammer, an inverted "T"), the hammer is placed into her lap for a moment. This is done to assure fertility in the marriage.

- A key part of the ceremony is to have the groom ceremonially give the bride a set of keys, which symbolize her receipt of responsibility for the home and finances of the family and invokes the power of Frigg.

- In modern Heathenism, the bride would typically reciprocate with the gifting of the groom with an

---

[56] http://members.iquest.net/~chaviland/asatru_wedding.html

heirloom weapon such as a sword or axe symbolizing that he is responsible for protecting the family. Because few modern households posses an heirloom sword to pass down, most heathen brides to be purchase an heirloom-quality sword for this purpose.

- There is occasionally a portion of the service in which the groom's kinsmen wrest the bride from the bride's family, either by staging a mock struggle for her, or by threatening anyone in the crowd should they be considering threatening the conclusion of the ceremony.

- Like almost all weddings, costuming for the wedding party is an important part of the festivities. The bride will often wear a reconstructed viking women's dress with over-apron and twin turtle brooches, and the groom a tunic and trews. The bride often wears an amber necklace representing Freyja's tears, and the man wearing a token of his faith such as a hammer or volknut pendant.

- Like all heathen ceremonies, the drinking horn is key part, with the couple sharing a draft of mead from the same horn. In ancient times, it was a sign of marriage or courtship for the couple to drink from the same vessel, and for the man and woman to feed each other choice bits from the same trencher or plate. Thus, they will usually follow the modern tradition of feeding each other a bit of bread or wedding cake to honor that ancient tradition as well. Mead, is of course the traditional beverage for this occasion - to honor the ancient *honey*moon tradition from which this derives.

- Music is often a part of the modern ceremony, with some traditional pieces such as the Bridal Chorus from Wagner's Loengrin being ver common.

A basic example framework for a heathen wedding

1. The Gothi performs a hammer working or similar blessing for the space around the area where the wedding is to take place. This may be done prior to the arrival of the wedding party and guests.

2. It is often a good idea, when the marriage service will be attended by folks who are unfamiliar with our ways, to have the Gothi say some words about the ceremony, its ancient roots, and the traditional symbolism of the ceremony. This helps to place the ceremony into perspective, and to tie it to the kinds of weddings they will undoubtedly have seen before.

3. The Groom's party comes into the area in reverse order, with the best man followed by the groom last. If they are carrying swords, they may choose to

present arms in a formal fashion.

4. The bride's party comes in while a processional music plays. Again the bride will be last, and ideally she will be escorted by her father. If the groomsmen are armed, I have seen them make an arch of swords for the bride's party to walk through.

5. The father gives the bride to the groom and takes his seat.

6. It is traditional in the United States to give the audience a chance to object to the union at some point early in the wedding ceremony. Because marriage in Viking times was in part sanctioned by the community, this is harks back to that.

7. A symbolic gesture showing the union of the couple is often done here - like tying the hands of the bride and groom to each other.

8. The ceremonial eating of the cake/bread and drinking of the mead might take place at this point.

9. The exchange of the keys and sword might occur next.

10. The blessing of the bride with hammer fits in nicely here...

11. The formal announcement of the marriage and the tradition kissing of the bride is a great way to finish off the wedding ceremony, with the grand processional of the wedding party out of the immediate area afterwards.

12. In most weddings, the bride and groom then shake hands with the attendees in a formal receiving line after all this

Profession[57]

To Profess one's belief in and kinship to the Gods is a turning point in ones life. The ritual itself is actually quite simple and can even be done during a blot.

The Gothi stands in front of the altar and says "Will [insert name here] please come forward." After he or she does so "Are you here of your own free will? Is it your intention to solemnly swear allegiance and kinship to the Gods of Asgard, the Aesir and Vanir?" If the answer to both these questions is in the affirmative the Gothi takes up the oath ring and holds it out to the person professing and says "Repeat after me. I swear to ever follow the way of the North, to always act with honor and bravery, and to be ever true to the Aesir and Vanir. By the gods I so swear. By my honor I so swear. On this Holy Ring I so swear. Hail the Gods." Everyone then replies "Hail the Gods!" and the Gothi finishes "Then be welcome to the service of Asgard and to our community."

The essence of Profession is making a commitment to heathenism. It should not be undertaken without thought and prayer. When one Professes, one is leaving behind other faiths. If one isn't yet comfortable in doing this, then Profession should be put off, perhaps indefinitely. It should

---

57 http://www.ravenkindred.com/RBRituals.html

be reiterated here that there should be absolutely no pressure put on people to Profess. False or coerced Professions merely cheapen the ritual and the commitment that it represents. It should also be said that Asatru ritual is open to anyone. You do not need to have undergone a ritual of Profession in order to attend kindred events or worship the Gods.

Funeral

Cattle die, kindred die,
Every man is mortal:
But the good name never dies
Of one who has done well

Cattle die, kindred die,
Every man is mortal:
But I know one thing that never dies,
The glory of the great dead[58]

While historically we know more about burial practices of the vikings than weddings, however we don't know much about the funerals themselves. Chris Havaland has developed an excellent set of considerations for heathen funerals.[59]

The following contains common elements in a modern heathen funeral service. Death, like life, is as varied and multi-faceted as any human experience, and each funeral service should be tailored to the specific requirements of the situation.

General Considerations:

    1. First, remember that heathenism is a religion of the

---

58 The Havamal
59 http://members.iquest.net/~chaviland/Basic_funeral_elements.htm

living. As such, funeral services are for the living as much as they are for the dead. Consider the needs of the living that will attend the service when constructing the service. For example, if the service is primarily for the comrades of the deceased (such as a military group) - you may wish to emphasize the heroic elements of death, whereas if it is a service for a young child the message should more of comfort and the continuity of the soul.

2. Second, heathenism is a religion of deeds, and remembering the deeds of the individual should form a large part of the service.
3. Third, heathens do not fear death as there is no evil to torture them in the afterlife, only rest, joy, and healing. It is living that is hard, much of what comes to man cannot be prepared for or avoided - only met honorably and with determination.
4. Determine the desires of the deceased with regard to inhumation or cremation - when depositing grave goods, it is important to know how they will be used. For inhumation, the goods will typically be buried with the deceased, and the deceased should be groomed (preferably by his or her family) and arrayed in clothing they loved, with grave goods arrayed about them. These goods should/could include: swords, weapons and/or tools that they have

had a high affinity for, domestic equipage, food, a drinking implement like a horn, jewelry, and the like. In the case of a cremation, the grave goods should be burned and interred with the remains, or else buried with them. If the body cannot be recovered, the goods may be ceremonially deposited in a bog or burned and buried.

5. A Thors hammer must be given to the earth, buried, or burned for every heathen funeral. This is the symbol of our faith, regardless of the individual's affinity for another deity, and a potent symbol of hallowing and rebirth.
6. Ideally, a rune stone or graver marker should be raised for the deceased - in the Viking age this was done rarely, and only for those who merited it. In the case of a soldier killed in war, this is the highest honor that can be paid them. A rune stone can be raised many years after the funeral.
7. Music can be a powerful part of the funeral experience. There are many fine modern Scandinavian recordings that convey the sadness of a funeral. If the deceased was particularly fond of certain folk music, a selection of these should be played.

Basic Elements:

1. Hallowing - The space in which the funeral is to take place should be hallowed with a hammer. Particularly, the body of the deceased must be hammer signed if it is present.
2. Introduction - If non-heathens are present at the funeral, it is desirable to place the ceremony into context. This should be tailored to the life and wishes of the deceased.
3. Reading - Typically, a portion of the Poetic Edda is read to open the memorial portion of the service - most often, Havamal 76 is read:
"Cattle die, kinsmen die,
one day you die yourself;
I know one thing that never dies-
the dead man's reputation."
4. Memorial - People who have known the deceased should stand before the group and speak about the life and deeds of the deceased. Ideally, this is done by raising a cup and drinking a toast to the their memory. In an intimate setting, a horn or cup might be passed around and everyone speaks about the deceased or simply toasts them. It is appropriate at this point if the deceased left significant unfinished work or responsibilities behind them for their

friends and family to give oath to see those responsibilities completed in their name. For example, if they leave a wife and children behind, it is appropriate to take oath to see them cared for, It is meet and fitting that those gathered sing songs about the deceased composed for the occasion, laugh at remembered moments, cry tears at their loss, recite poetry they loved - in short, to remember them well.
5. Final Prayer – A final prayer should be said after the toasts.

    6. Closing - It is desirable at this point to say a few words to close the ceremony. A simple statement of love and respect that underscores the eternal nature of the soul and life is appropriate here. At a minimum, close the ceremony with the phrase: "The rite is ended, but the folk go on". Below find an example of a generic closing statement:

    "We will never forget you and we will always love you. We wish you peace and healing. Come back to us when you're ready - and until we meet again, rest safe and sound in hands of the Gods. Farewell! The rite is ended, but the folk go on."

In Conclusion

I hope you've enjoyed reading this book as much as I've enjoyed writing it. Over the last dozen years I've officiated at and been present at dozens, if not hundreds of blots. Each one has its own color, its own mood, and its own result. What I've given you here is a place to start, and some ideas. However now its upon you to take what you've read here and make it your own. I hope you'll choose to share that, and to share what you've experienced with others. Its only through sharing with our community do we truly grow.

So go out, perform those blots. Invite other people that you may barely know and share with them the joy of what it means to be "heathen." Its a path that is filled with not just great difficulty, but also of great joy. These rituals, and the ones you create, are part of that celebration of our beliefs. They bring us closer to the gods, and share with them the joy in the life we are living.

Scott Mohnkern

aka The Modern Heathen

http://www.modernheathen.com

Made in the USA
Middletown, DE
25 May 2021